A TIME BOMB LIES BURIED
Fiji's Road to Independence, 1960-1970

Brij V. Lal

State, Society and Governance in Melanesia
Monograph, No. 1

E PRESS

Published by ANU E Press
The Australian National University
Canberra ACT 0200, Australia
Email: anuepress@anu.edu.au
This title is also available online at: http://epress.anu.edu.au/time_bomb_citation.html

---

National Library of Australia
Cataloguing-in-Publication entry

Author: Lal, Brij V.
Title: A time bomb lies buried : Fiji's road to independence,
                 1960-1970 / author, Brij V. Lal.
Publisher: Acton, A.C.T. : ANU E Press, 2008.
ISBN: 9781921313608 (pbk.)
                 9781921313615 (web)
Series: Studies in state and society in the Pacific
Subjects: Fiji--History--Autonomy and independence movements
                 Fiji--Politics and government--20th century.
                 Fiji--History--20th century.
Dewey Number: 996.11

All rights reserved. No part of this publication may be reproduced, stored in a retrieval system or transmitted in any form or by any means, electronic, mechanical, photocopying or otherwise, without the prior permission of the publisher.

This book has been published on the recommendation of the Pacific Editorial Board, which is convened by the Pacific Centre.

Cover design by ANU E Press

This edition © 2008 ANU E Press

Table of Contents

Acknowledgment	vii
About the Author	ix
1. Introduction	1
2. Paramountcy, Parity, Privilege	9
3. Amery and the Aftermath	25
4. The 1965 Constitutional Conference	49
5. Towards Independence	67
Afterword	83
Appendix 1. Policy in Fiji (Nov. 1960)	91
Leg. Co. and Ex. Co.	92
The Public Service	93
The Fijian Administration	93
Appendix 2. Fiji Final Dispatch (8 Oct. 1970)	95

Acknowledgment

I wish to thank Stephen Ashton, General Editor of the *British Documents on the end of Empire* project, for inviting me to edit the Fiji volume for the series; the ever courteous people at the Public Records Office at Kew Gardens for their assistance in accessing the records; the Institute of Commonwealth Studies, for a Senior Research Fellowship, at the University of London where some of this work was written; the Division of Pacific and Asian History at The Australian National University for granting me leave to undertake the project; and Stephen Ashton, Robert Norton, Rod Alley, Stewart Firth and Jon Fraenkel for reading a draft and making many helpful suggestions for revision. The usual disclaimer applies.

About the Author

Brij V. Lal is a Professor of Pacific and Asian History in the Research School of Pacific and Asian Studies at The Australian National University. He has published widely on the history and politics of his native Fiji and on the history and culture of the Indian diaspora. His latest book is *Islands of Turmoil: Elections and Politics in Fiji* and, as co-editor, *1987 and All That: Fiji Twenty Years On*. He was a member of the three-person Fiji Constitution Review Commission whose report formed the basis of Fiji's present (1997) multiracial constitution.

1. Introduction

In his Christmas message to the people of Fiji, Governor Sir Kenneth Maddocks described 1961 as a year of 'peaceful progress'.[1] The memory of industrial disturbance and a brief period of rioting and looting in Suva in 1959 was fading rapidly.[2] The nascent trade union movement, multi-ethnic in character, which had precipitated the strike, was beginning to fracture along racial lines. The leading Fijian chiefs, stunned by the unexpectedly unruly behaviour of their people, warned them against associating with people of other races, emphasising the importance of loyalty to the Crown and respect for law and order.[3] The strike in the sugar industry, too, was over. Though not violent in character, the strike had caused much damage to an economy dependent on sugar, it bitterly split the Indo-Fijian community and polarised the political atmosphere.[4] A commission of inquiry headed by Sir Malcolm Trustram Eve (later Lord Silsoe) was appointed to investigate the causes of the dispute and to recommend a new contract between the growers, predominantly Indo-Fijians, and the monopoly miller, the Australian Colonial Sugar Refining Company (CSR). The recommendations of the Burns Commission — as it came to be known, after its chairman, the former governor of the Gold Coast (Ghana), Sir Alan Burns — into the natural resources and population of Fiji were being scrutinised by the government.[5] The construction of roads, bridges, wharves, schools, hospital buildings and water supply schemes was moving apace. The governor had good reason to hope for 'peaceful progress'.

Rather more difficult was the issue of political reform, but the governor's message announced that constitutional changes would be introduced. The existing constitution, in place since 1937, had been overtaken by immense social, economic and demographic change in the postwar years.[6] The international climate had also changed during this time. Former colonies in Asia and Africa had gained, or were in the process of gaining, independence.[7] Harold Macmillan's 'winds of change' were gaining momentum everywhere. After Hong Kong, Fiji was Britain's last major colonial dependency in the East Asia-Pacific region. Whitehall was keen to avoid being overtaken by events. It hoped to lead Fiji to internal self-government if not to full independence perhaps over a decade of cautious, gradual reform. The constitutional settlement aimed for had to be broadly acceptable to all the people of the colony as well as to the international community — but especially to the indigenous Fijians, for reasons that will become clear shortly. The governor informed the Legislative Council that its size would be increased from 15 to 18 unofficial members, consisting of six Europeans, six Fijians and six Indo-Fijians. Four members of each community would be elected from separate communal rolls and two nominated by the governor. In the case of Fijians, the two members would be chosen by the Great

Council of Chiefs. The number of official members would be 19. Women would be extended franchise for the first time and the property qualification for voters abolished. The government hoped for a slow but steady start to assuage the fears and anxieties of all the segments of Fiji's society.

Therein lay the problem that would preoccupy Suva and London for the rest of the decade, until Fiji finally gained independence in 1970. Fiji was a colony not of 'one people' but of three separate ethnic groups, each with its own distinctive understanding of its interests and aspirations in the broad scheme of things, its own distinctive historical experience and economic circumstances.[8] For one group, the Indo-Fijians, the pace of change was not rapid enough. They rejected the premises that underpinned the racially ordered political structure that Suva proposed and London reluctantly acquiesced to, and wanted it replaced with one that was racially neutral. In other words, they wanted a common-roll system of voting, not a communal system. Further, they saw any constitutional advance towards greater internal self-governance as leading inevitably and desirably to full independence in the not too distant future. If Western Samoa could become independent in 1962 and Cook Islands could attain full internal self-government in free association with New Zealand in 1965, why not Fiji, they argued (somewhat misleadingly) as Fiji, by virtue of its history and demography, was unique in the Pacific.

This view was rejected by the Europeans and Fijians. They insisted on the full and complete retention of the racial system of voting and guaranteed equal political representation for the three main groups, irrespective of population size. This guaranteed representation, it was feared, would be jeopardised in an open, non-racial system of voting, which, in their view, would lead to uncertainty and unrestrained competition for power. Since Indo-Fijians were the majority community, an open, racially neutral system would lead to 'Indian domination'. That outcome would be unpalatable at any cost, a sure recipe for disaster, perhaps even racial violence. Furthermore, Fijians and Europeans did not want links with the British Crown severed. They saw no reason for that. Unlike the Indo-Fijians, they instead wanted them strengthened.

London's dilemma was thus starkly defined. The prospect of independence could not be ignored, however much significant numbers of Fijians and Europeans opposed it. Nor could the UK government ignore the increasingly insistent and sometimes politically embarrassing demands for decolonisation from the United Nations' Committee of Twenty-Four.[9] Western Samoa's independence from New Zealand in 1962 was followed by that of tiny Nauru from Australia, in 1968.[10] By the early 1960s, the question was not whether Fiji would become independent; that was a foregone conclusion. Indeed, as Roderic Alley has pointed out, the paradox of decolonisation in Fiji 'was further underlined by British attempts, throughout the 1960s, to encourage the growth of representative political organisations likely to responsibly contest office and hasten decolonisation'.[11]

The real and the most fraught question was on what — or whose — terms would independence be achieved. The Colonial Office (CO) acknowledged the substance and the logic of the non-racial argument, and accepted the imperative to create, as far as possible, political institutions that were based on ideology, not race; however, its hands were tied. Officials had a prudent appreciation of the strength and character of the Fijian opposition to any change that might unwittingly give the impression of derogating from their privileged position in the colony. Fijians constituted the overwhelming majority of the colony's armed forces, a key fact that could not be ignored, or ignored at the government's peril. Moreover, there were many influential officials in London and in Suva who felt a keen sense of moral responsibility to hand the colony back to the people — the indigenous Fijians — who had ceded it to Her Majesty Queen Victoria in the first place and who had, in war and in peace, remained steadfastly loyal and respectful to the Crown.

This essay attempts to present as full an account as possible of the political dilemmas that Suva and London faced in deciding the future course of Fiji's constitutional evolution, and chronicles the ideas, issues, assumptions, understandings and internal debates that determined policy. Several points need to be emphasised. The documents on which this essay is based emphasise the concerns and priorities of the UK government, informed closely as they were by regular reports from Fiji. I have immersed myself in the Fijian side of this story as much as is possible, though it has to be said that sensitive documents on the period are not always found in the archives. More likely, they are to be located in disorganised and decaying private collections of the leading players of the day. Fortunately for the researcher, the most important documents (the Wakaya Letter, for example) or the substance of private conversation on controversial topics (such as the negotiations preceding the 1965 constitutional conference) were leaked to the newspapers or raised in political rallies. Local sources, where they can be located, can be useful in supplying colour and detail, but little of importance escaped London's notice. Some sources, such as the reports of the Fiji Intelligence Committee, are not found in Suva, but a complete set exists in London. The CO documents provide, without question, the most complete picture of the nature of political debate for the period.

There was broad agreement among top policy makers in Suva and London but by no means complete consensus on all major issues in dispute. On the contrary, the records show how widely divergent the views sometimes were and how, over time, they were developed through endless minutes into a coherent policy. Nor was there unanimity of opinion between London and Suva over what the most appropriate course of action might be. London listened and consulted closely with the governor, paid close attention to his assessment of the situation on the ground, and sought his opinion and even initiative on important matters. There was hardly a policy of importance on which the governor was not consulted, although his views were refined or modified — sometimes even rejected — in the light of the wider experience in London.

A typical way in which policy was developed might follow this pattern. The governor would inform London of a particular issue or problem he had under consideration. This might be communicated through a letter or a telegram. It was sent after the governor had full consultation with his senior advisors, whose advice guided but did not necessarily confine the governor to a particular course of action or line of thought. On political and constitutional matters, the recipient in Whitehall was invariably the head of the Pacific and Indian Ocean Department, initially at the CO (until 1966, when the head was an assistant secretary). The CO then merged with the Commonwealth Relations Office to form the Commonwealth Office (1966–68), which in turn merged with the Foreign Office to form the Foreign and Commonwealth Office (FCO)(from October 1968). At the CO, the communication would be the subject of internal debate or discussion through a series of internal departmental minutes and meetings. Other CO departments, or other government departments outside the CO, were brought in when needed. Within the CO, the discussion proceeded up a chain of command to a supervising assistant undersecretary responsible for several departments, including the Pacific and Indian Ocean, and then, on matters of the highest importance, to the permanent undersecretary, the senior CO official.

Ministerial involvement in Fiji's affairs was usually conducted at a level beneath that of secretary of state. While some secretaries of state visited Fiji as part of wider Pacific tours (Fred Lee from the CO in 1966 and Herbert Bowden from the Commonwealth Office in 1967), in London it was more usual for junior ministers — specifically the parliamentary undersecretary of state at the CO, and the minister of state at the Commonwealth Office and the FCO — to take responsibility for Fiji. Junior ministers were also visitors to Fiji. Julian Amery's 1960 visit as parliamentary undersecretary at the CO had significant long-term political consequences. Other junior ministers playing important but lesser roles were Nigel Fisher and Eirene White in 1963 and 1965 respectively, both as parliamentary undersecretaries at the CO, and Lord Shepherd, minister of state at the FCO. Shepherd was especially important at the time of Fiji's independence, visiting the colony shortly beforehand and presiding over the independence conference in London. Only rarely did the secretaries of state become involved with Fiji — a reflection, it must be said, of where Fiji ranked in UK priorities. Although Fiji was by some distance the most important of the United Kingdom's Pacific possessions — possessing what London viewed as an acute and potentially dangerous racial problem — it was still, in contrast with other territories (Aden and British Guiana, for example) relatively peaceful. To the extent that secretaries of state involved themselves, it was usually in the context of where Fiji stood in relation to UK policy towards remaining dependent territories as a group. Communications were often sent back to Suva in the name of the secretary of state but junior ministers and senior officials were the real policy makers. Other cabinet ministers were hardly ever brought in, although, as was always the case before independence, Fiji had to be placed on the agenda of the Cabinet's influential Defence and Overseas Policy Committee. And policy towards Fiji did not change with a change of government in the United Kingdom. The policies on Fiji of the Conservative governments, to October 1964, and then from June 1970 until independence in October of the same year, and the Labour governments between 1964 and 1970 (an election in 1966 gave Labour an increased majority) were indistinguishable. The point was not appreciated sufficiently by some leaders in Fiji, particularly on the Indo-Fijian side, who expected from a Labour government a more sympathetic understanding of their cause and concerns.

Once a policy was communicated to the governor — and if the subject involved a significant constitutional change — an outline text was published in London as a white paper. These and their Suva counterparts are available widely. The documents referred to here are from the Public Records Office at Kew Gardens. Overwhelmingly, the documents I have drawn on are from two main classes at the National Archives (UK): CO 1036, the records of the Colonial and Commonwealth Office from the Pacific and Indian Ocean Department, 1952–67, and FCO 32, the successor Pacific and Indian Ocean Department of the Commonwealth Office and FCO from 1967 to 1974.

This essay — like the volume of documents to which it relates — focuses on the period 1960–70. With Fiji's independence in 1970, Britain's formal responsibility for the colony ceased, although there were continuing consultations about defence and related matters. The essay opens in 1960 because that was when the first serious discussion started about the future course of Fiji's constitutional development, and when the first policies toward greater internal self-government were enunciated. The decade was dominated in Fiji by intense, often deeply bitter, debate about decolonisation, especially about the way in which Fijian interests — accepted by everyone as special and requiring specific, watertight protection — could be safeguarded in any future constitutional arrangement within a framework that was, to all outward appearances, democratic and acceptable to the international community. The faint outline of what eventually transpired began to become visible by 1965, and clarified as the decade progressed.

Constitutional matters had been very much on the mind of Sir Ronald Garvey, Maddocks' predecessor as governor, throughout the 1950s. Garvey was an independent-minded old Pacific hand, having served from the late 1920s in a number of locations, including the Solomon Islands, where he was district officer (1927–32), and then Nyasaland, St Vincent in the Caribbean and British Honduras (as governor, 1948–52) before becoming governor of Fiji in 1952.[12] From very early in his tenure as governor, he was concerned that Fiji's constitutional arrangements had become an obstacle to the colony's political progress and an impediment to harmonious race relations. From the mid-1950s onwards, Garvey proposed a number of constitutional reforms, none of which bore fruit during his time in Fiji because they were deemed premature, too far ahead of public opinion, or insufficiently cognisant of the constraints of the colony's complex and contested history; some of them would, however, be revisited a decade later only to show Garvey's farsightedness. Garvey was concerned also with the internal social and economic problems facing the Fijian people and with the problems hindering the economic advancement of Fiji. He took measures to address these issues, which came to the fore by the late 1950s and which would have important implications for social and political issues that dominated the 1960s. While the 1960s is the principal focus of this essay, events taking place during that time, the issues that divided the people and confounded senior officials in London and Suva, had deep roots in Fiji's colonial history. It is to these that we now turn.

ENDNOTES

[1] *Fiji: Report for the Year 1961*, 1962, Her Majesty's Stationery Service, London, p. 5.

[2] For an account of the strike, see Rutherford, Noel 1984, 'The 1959 Strike', in N. Rutherford and P. Hempenstall (eds), *Protest and Dissent in the Colonial Pacific*, Institute of Pacific Studies, Suva, pp. 73–86. The official report into the inquiry, 'Report of Commission of Inquiry into the Disturbances in Suva, December 1959', is in *Fiji Legislative Council Paper*, no. 10/1960.

[3] For more details, see Lal, Brij V. 1992, *Broken Waves: A History of the Fiji Islands in the 20th Century*, University of Hawai'i Press, Honolulu, pp. 164–9. Ratu Mara was reported widely to have said after the 1959 disturbances that if Suva burned to the ground, the only thing the Fijian community would lose would be the record of their debts.

[4] An account of this strike is contained in Lal, Brij V. 1997a, *A Vision for Change: A. D. Patel and the Politics of Fiji*, National Centre for Development Studies, The Australian National University, Canberra, pp. 133–58. The strike split the Indo-Fijian community between the majority, who wanted to continue it, and the powerful minority who wanted it to end.

[5] See 'Report of the Commission of Enquiry into the Natural Resources and Population Trends of the Colony of Fiji 1959', published as *Legislative Council Paper*, no. 1/1960.

[6] There is no satisfactory account of this subject, but see Stanner, W. E. H. 1953, *The South Seas in Transition: A Study of Post-War Rehabilitation and Reconstruction in Three British Pacific Dependencies*, Australasian Publishing Company, Sydney.

[7] See Jeffrey, Robin 1970, *Asia: The Winning of Independence*, Macmillan, London.

[8] The 'three Fijis' concept was given scholarly expression by Fisk, E. K. 1970, *The Political Economy of Independent Fiji*, Australian National University Press, Canberra.

[9] The Committee of Twenty-Four—so named because of the number of members on it—was created by the UN General Assembly to implement its declaration on decolonisation. The committee drew a large number of its members from formerly colonised countries.

[10] For a succinct survey, see Davidson, J. W. 1971, 'The Decolonisation of Oceania', *Journal of Pacific History*, vol. 6, pp. 133–50. See also Larmour, Peter 1983, 'The Decolonisation of the Pacific', in R. Crocombe and A. Ali (eds), *Foreign Forces in Pacific Politics*, Institute of Pacific Studies, Suva, pp. 1–25.

[11] Alley, Roderic 1986, 'The Emergence of Party Politics', in B. V. Lal (ed.), *Politics in Fiji: Studies in Contemporary History*, Allen and Unwin, Sydney, p. 29.

[12] He would leave Fiji in 1958 to become Governor of the Isle of Man, from which post he retired in 1966.

2. Paramountcy, Parity, Privilege

An archipelago of some 300 islands lying on the border between the cultural regions of Melanesia and Polynesia, Fiji was settled about 3,000 years ago by a seafaring people travelling eastwards from the Southeast Asian region.[1] The population was made up of a number of rival, semi-autonomous tribal chiefdoms embroiled in incessant struggle for political supremacy. The problem of power struggle was compounded by the arrival of European traders, beachcombers, missionaries and fortune seekers from the beginning of the nineteenth century. They took sides among the rival aspirants, acquired land through dubious means, built up plantations, engaged in trading (in sandalwood, bêche-de-mer, coconut oil, shipping), created port towns and urban centres and variously sought to insert themselves into the political scene, creating mayhem in the process.[2] Unable to tame these new, destabilising forces of change and fearing for their own political fortunes, the leading chiefs of Fiji, headed by Ratu Seru Cakobau — the self-styled *Tui Viti*, the supreme chief of the archipelago — ceded Fiji to the United Kingdom on 10 October 1874.[3] Britain accepted the offer after spurning earlier ones, now keen to exercise control over the activities of its restive nationals on the unsettled island frontier and to heed calls by missionaries and other humanitarians to curb abuses in the Pacific island labour traffic, which was reported to be soaked in innocent blood.[4]

The transfer of sovereignty was cemented through a Deed of Cession. Much has been made of the deed and it certainly featured prominently in the constitutional debates of the 1960s. The Fijian leaders invested it with a particular meaning. The deed, they argued, assured them not only that their rights and privileges would be safeguarded by the Crown, but that they would remain paramount in the management of the colony's affairs. 'Paramountcy of Fijian interests' was a phrase invoked over and over again throughout the 1960s to stake special claims and to influence the direction of constitutional change.[5] Some Fijian leaders even asserted that in its intent and implication, the Deed of Cession was similar to the Treaty of Waitangi under which the Maori ceded sovereignty of New Zealand to the United Kingdom. The comparison is misleading. Unlike New Zealand, which was a settler colony (while Fiji was a Crown colony), the cession of sovereignty was recognised and enforced in law, a fact that had 'never been questioned or even raised as an issue'.[6]

The words of the deed in English — there was no vernacular version,[7] unlike the Treaty of Waitangi — are clear. The chiefs who ceded Fiji to the United Kingdom agreed that the 'possession of and full sovereignty and dominion over the whole of the group of islands in the South Pacific Ocean known as the Fijis' were to be 'annexed to and be a possession of and dependency of the British

Crown', that the Crown would 'prescribe and determine' the laws and legislation governing the colony, that the

> absolute proprietorship of all lands not shown to be now alienated so as to have become bona fide property of Europeans or other foreigners or not now in the actual use or occupation of some Chief or tribe or not actually required for the probable future support and maintenance of some chief or tribe shall be and is hereby declared to be vested in Her said Majesty her heirs and successors.

That is, it would become Crown land. Finally, the deed acknowledged that on cession, 'the rights and interests of the said Tui Viti and other high chiefs ceding parties hereto shall be recognised so far as is and shall be consistent with British Sovereignty and Colonial form of government'.[8] That was the extent of the undertaking given in the deed, and it was endorsed by such Indo-Fijian leaders as A. D. Patel and Vishnu Deo in the 1940s.

The phrase 'paramountcy of Fijian interests' entered Fiji's political vocabulary in the early twentieth century, often invoked by European settlers as guardians of the 'Fijian race' to protect the European-dominated colonial order against demands by Indo-Fijians for constitutional change. Political and economic self-interest rather than a genuine desire to protect Fijian interests informed the European reading of the document — for the same people who championed the cause of the Fijians hankered for more Fijian labour and land, some even going to the extent of seeking Fiji's federation with New Zealand because Fiji's laws protected the interests of the indigenous Fijians in a manner in which New Zealand labour laws did not protect Maori interests. The Fijians themselves saw the deed as a 'protective' document that would safeguard their 'rights and interests', particularly the ownership of land and chiefly titles. In that sense, their interests would be paramount. As independence approached, however, and fears were raised about how or if Fijian interests would receive special recognition in the new constitutional order, a protective interpretation was transformed into an 'assertive' one. That is, Fijian interests could be protected — be paramount — only if Fijians were in control of Fiji's political leadership, notwithstanding the legal and institutional protection. The deed, in other words, became a bulwark against change not authorised by or acceptable to the Fijian leaders.

Once Fiji was acquired, the first substantive governor, Sir Arthur Hamilton Gordon (1875–80), decided early that Fijian society, already showing signs of stress from contact with the outside world — the indigenous population had declined from about 200,000 at the time of cession to approximately 87,000 at the turn of the twentieth century, largely because of introduced diseases to which the people had no immunity — should be allowed to live within their own subsistence environment, under the leadership of their traditional chiefs in a system of indirect rule.[9] To that end, he created a separate system of native administration complete with its own rules and regulations and courts governing indigenous life, a system of native taxation through which people paid tax in kind rather than cash (thus preventing the disruption of the people's subsistence lifestyle), and engineered an inquiry into land alienation that eventually ensured that fully 83 per cent of all land would remain inalienably in Fijian ownership.[10] Fijian fears of dispossession of the kind that took place in other colonies — notably New Zealand — were by this process put to rest. The imposition of a uniform pattern of land ownership over an archipelago of great cultural and social diversity created its own problems,[11] but in the end, the Fijian people retained possession of most of their land. Now that the former Crown lands have been transferred to Fijian ownership, close to 90 per cent of all land is in Fijian hands.[12]

Gordon gave further substance to the idea of indirect rule by formalising, in 1876, a Council of Chiefs — an umbrella organisation of the indigenous community, comprising entirely chiefs until the 1940s — to advise him on all major policy matters relating to their people.[13] Although the strength and intensity of the consultative process fluctuated as times changed and other imperatives intruded, or when governors of a more reforming zeal were at the helm, the voice of the council was heard when and where it mattered. The Council of Chiefs was the only body in Fiji that enjoyed the honour of addressing the Crown directly, and this it did regularly, raising the concerns of the Fijian people or directing attention to matters that needed addressing. In the independence constitution, the Great Council of Chiefs, through its nominees in the Senate, was given the power of veto over all legislation that specifically affected Fijian interests. The 1997 constitution recognises the council as a constitutional body and gives it the power to nominate the president and the vice-president of the republic.

The United Kingdom acquired Fiji reluctantly for strategic purposes. The islands were remote and their economic potential unpromising. Unwilling to incur a heavy expenditure in starting the new colonial project, Britain expected the new colony to become economically self-sustaining in the quickest possible time. This was easier said than done, for the basic prerequisites for rapid economic development were lacking. Local Europeans — themselves insolvent after the collapse of the cotton boom after the end of the American civil war — could not be expected to provide capital sufficient for the large-scale plantation enterprise Gordon had in mind, having observed its success in Mauritius and Trinidad, where he was governor before coming to Fiji. Gordon settled on sugar cane as the crop most appropriate for Fiji, and turned to the Australian Colonial Sugar Refining Company.[14] The CSR arrived in Fiji in 1882 and remained there until 1973, dominating the colony's largely mono-crop economy and exercising great influence on the way matters were run. The company's determination to maintain an iron grip on the industry caused friction with the growers and occasionally colonial governors and led to three major strikes in the sugar industry in 1921, 1943 and in 1960 — although, not least for its own interests, the company was nevertheless a benevolent landlord. The conflict between the Indo-Fijian cane growers and the CSR would exercise a deep influence on political developments in Fiji in the post-World War II years.

The Indo-Fijian cane growers were descendants of indentured labourers. Gordon decided to introduce Indian indentured labour to Fiji because he had seen its success in Trinidad and Mauritius, where the first Indian migrants had gone in the 1830s. The prohibition on the commercial employment of Fijian labour on European plantations and the uncertainty of labour supply from the neighbouring Pacific islands necessitated the colony's dependence on India. Between 1879 and 1916, more than 60,000 indentured labourers were introduced into Fiji, 45,000 from north India and the remainder from the south after 1903.[15] Small groups of free migrants from Gujarat and the Punjab — later to become economically and politically significant — continued to join them after the formal abolition of indenture in 1920. The indentured migrants arrived on a five-year contract that promised a return passage at their own expense after five years of service or free passage after 10. For a variety of social and economic reasons — including inducement provided by the government to stay on — the majority of the migrants settled in Fiji and contributed immensely to the economic development of the colony. From the very beginning, it was expected that those who remained in Fiji as British subjects would enjoy rights equal to those enjoyed by other British subjects resident in the colony. This intention was encapsulated broadly in Lord Salisbury's dispatch of 1875,[16] even though it became a dead letter when Indian provincial governments refused the request to assist indentured recruitment and emigration. Nonetheless, the sentiment was repeated on many occasions later.[17] It was no doubt on the promise of equality that Indo-Fijians demanded full participation in the colony's political life. This demand for equality, too, would be at the core of the political debate as Fiji inched towards independence. Just as Fijians demanded the recognition of the principle of paramountcy, Indo-Fijian leaders struggled to gain acceptance of the principle of parity.

The third leg of the Fijian stool was the Europeans — which in Fiji included Australians, New Zealanders and British.[18] They had been coming to Fiji since the middle of the nineteenth century, numbering about 2000 at the time of cession. Although small in number, the Europeans dominated the retail and wholesale trade in the colony, owned or leased plantations and occupied senior positions in Fiji's public life. In keeping with the ethos of the times, they regarded themselves, by virtue of their 'race', as superior to other segments of the society and therefore entitled to a privileged position in the colony's affairs. In the late nineteenth and early twentieth centuries, European settlers, unhappy with the government's 'native' or land policies and unable to get their way, led a movement to federate Fiji with New Zealand. When that effort failed, they used other methods to gain recognition for their interests, chief of which was acceptance of their 'privileged' position in the colony's affairs.

Paramountcy, parity and privilege, then, were the three competing — not to say incompatible, but mutually reinforcing[19] — principles that informed the understanding the three communities had of their role and place in Fiji's society. These were invoked, at various times with varying degrees of success, whenever London and Suva mooted proposals for further constitutional change. The demand for changing the fundamental structure of the colonial order could be — and was — deflected as long as Suva and London had their hands on the levers of power and portrayed themselves as impartial arbiters of the colony's best interests. The Crown could be trusted to be fair to all its subjects. As independence loomed, however, and the departure of the colonial government became a certainty, the feeling of comfort began to give way to a deep and disquieting concern about the values and assumptions that should underpin the new order and about how the vital interests of the three communities could best be protected. This would be the central issue facing the CO in the 1960s.

A colony deeply divided by ethnicity and competing claims to political representation was one reality that confronted London and Suva. There was another: the racially compartmentalised nature of the electoral system that Fiji had adopted from the outset. From cession in 1874 to 1904, the Legislative Council comprised members nominated by the governor, much to the dismay and opposition of the European settler community, which wanted direct (and greater) representation. Their continuing agitation had the effect of forcing Suva to open up the legislature to limited elected representation.[20] By Letters Patent of March 1904, the hitherto wholly nominated legislature was replaced with one comprising 10 official members, six elected Europeans and two Fijians nominated by the Council of Chiefs. In 1916, the Letters Patent were further revised, increasing European representation by one (from six to seven) and nominated members from 10 to 12, one of whom, for the first time, was an Indo-Fijian (Badri Maharaj). Fijian representation remained unchanged. In 1929, partly as a result of representation by the Government of India, the Letters Patent were once again revised, reducing European seats in the Legislative Council from seven to six, giving Indo-Fijians three seats, to be elected from a communal roll, and three to Fijians, to be selected by the governor from a list of names submitted by the Council of Chiefs. The new Legislative Council therefore consisted of 13 official members, 12 unofficial members, nine elected and three nominated.

Soon after election, the Indo-Fijian members walked out of the Legislative Council when their motion for a non-racial common-roll system of voting was rejected.[21] This was the first public occasion when the government's policy of separate racial representation was challenged, but not the last. The issue of common roll would become one of the most deeply divisive in Fijian politics in the 1960s. Throughout the early 1930s, the method of election — common roll versus communal roll — the disparity in the representation of the three communities and the merits of nomination over elected representation dominated the political debate in the colony.[22] Indo-Fijians demanded parity with the Europeans, while Fijians favoured nomination over election and rejected the Indo-Fijians' demands as unreasonable and unjustified and a threat to their own position in the colony. London refused consistently to sanction common roll, citing as its reason the need to uphold pledges given to the Fijian people in the Deed of Cession. Europeans and Fijians opposed common roll, which they saw as the thin end of the wedge for Indian domination, and both opposed the system of election, at least in part because they saw this as threatening their particular interests. The Europeans feared competition from the part-Europeans (as they were called) because the latter were greater — and rapidly increasing — in number, and Fijian chiefs opposed election because they saw it as a threat to their traditional way of life and because their key concern was the economic betterment of the Fijians, not national constitutional advancement.

Change could not, however, be averted. In 1937, the Letters Patent were amended. For the first time, the three main ethnic groups were given equal representation in the Legislative Council, with five members each. Three each of the Europeans and Indo-Fijians were to be elected — with property qualification for candidates and voters — from communal rolls and two nominated by the governor. For the Fijians, the governor nominated five members from a list of 10 submitted by the Council of Chiefs. The remainder of the Legislative Council was made up of 'official members' — that is, heads of government departments. The distribution of representation in the Legislative Council ensured that the government always had the numbers to carry the day even in the most unlikely event of all the non-official members combining against it. As Mellor and Anthony point out:

> The permanent official majority retained control over its proceedings, and the initiative for measures governing the conduct of the administration lay with its members. The prime role of the unofficial members, both elected and nominated, was to question and influence, hoping through reason and persuasion, to shape legislation and to fit the governmental activities of the colony to Fiji's needs.[23]

This structure remained in place until 1963.

It remained intact but not unchallenged. Throughout the 1940s and 1950s, unofficial members made several attempts — all ultimately unsuccessful — to persuade Suva (and through it London) to change policy and open up representation in the legislature to reflect and accommodate the demographic, social and economic changes sweeping Fiji, as well as to honour London's commitment to gradual self-government for the colonies. Specifically, the advocates of constitutional change wanted the system of nomination abolished and replaced by election. The agitation for constitutional reform in the 1940s was led not by the Indo-Fijian leaders but by Europeans. The main period of Indo-Fijian political agitation had ceased by the mid-1930s and would not be revived until the early 1960s. Unable to persuade their Fijian and European counterparts to embrace the principle of non-racialism, they quietly supported — but did not initiate — constitutional debate. For their part, Fijian leaders staunchly resisted any substantive change to the constitution, or any perceived dilution of their cherished links to the British Crown cemented in the Deed of Cession.

The first wartime debate took place in 1943, when Alport Barker, elected member of the Legislative Council and mayor of Suva, moved to have the nomination system abolished in favour of election, and to increase the number of unofficial members from five to six for each of the three main communities. His aim was to give the unofficial members dominance in the council. The debate went nowhere. Fiji was engaged in the Pacific War, and the sugar industry was embroiled in a catastrophic strike.[24] Barker withdrew the motion when the governor promised to appoint a select committee to investigate the issue.[25] Two years later, Harold Gibson, another elected member, broached the subject of increased elected representation — again to no avail. In 1948, Amie Ragg raised the subject again, but Fijians remained opposed. With the Indo-Fijian population becoming an outright majority in the colony, London and Suva expressed concern about the protection of the interests of the indigenous community. And this — together with a growing concern about how to deal with the 'Indian problem' — weighed heavily on the minds of officials. Opinion in Suva was divided. Some urged greater sympathy for the position of Indo-Fijians, who had made an enormous contribution to the economy and who had, therefore, their fair share of rights in the colony. They urged greater Fijian integration into the mainstream colonial economy.

In London, too, opinion was divided. Some officials urged caution and sympathy for the Fijian position. J. B. Sidebotham, assistant secretary and head of the then Pacific Department at the CO, was adamant that any attempt by Europeans and Indo-Fijians to force the pace of change should be 'firmly resisted', otherwise 'we are not fulfilling our duties as guardians' of the Fijian people.[26] Removing the official majority would place the Fijians at the mercy of Europeans and Indo-Fijians, 'who would undoubtedly use the resulting situation for their own ends'. And any change that disturbed the traditional nature of the political structure — elections, for example — would be 'the greatest disservice that we could do to the Fijians', because they would become the 'plaything of political parties of other races'. There were, however, also those who argued that the status quo could not continue indefinitely. Among them was Sir Charles Jeffries, joint deputy undersecretary of state at the CO, who responded that the system of electoral representation had to bear some resemblance to the size of the two communities:

> We cannot hope to hold indefinitely or perhaps for very long, the position that an official autocracy is necessary because the Fijian community is backward. We have to face the fact that the Fijians are only half the population of the Colony. The other half consists mainly of Indians, with a not negligible minority of whites. We, as trustees, have a special obligation to protect the interests of the Fijian race, but it is obvious that the ultimate goal must be a constitution based on a Fijian citizenship which shall include persons of all races who have made their home in the Colony.[27]

The 'no-changers' prevailed.

By the mid-1950s, Fiji had changed dramatically from the prewar years. In 1956, of the total colonial population of 345,164, Indo-Fijians numbered 48.2 per cent, Fijians 42.6 per cent, Europeans 2.7 per cent, part-Europeans 2.3 per cent, Chinese 1.2 per cent and other Pacific Islanders 3 per cent.[28] The increase in the Indo-Fijian population, which had overtaken the Fijian population during the war — increasing by 46,000 between 1945 and 1955 (it had taken Fijians 22 years to reach that figure) — was due mainly to four factors: a higher fertility rate, a lower infant mortality rate compared with the Fijians, the early marriage of Indo-Fijian women and a higher proportion of female children.[29] These figures rang many alarm bells. Population projections were disturbing. By 1967, it was predicted, the Indo-Fijian population would increase to one-quarter of a million while the Fijians would not reach that figure until 1980. The disparity in the real size as well as in the projection of Fijian and Indo-Fijian populations not only caused officials concern, it poisoned race relations in the colony, leading to calls in the 1950s for steady deportation of Indo-Fijians to remoter parts of the empire, such as the New Guinea highlands and even the Marquesas, which was a French territory!

There were other developments that were beginning to change the public face of the colony. As a result of the war, sea and air communication had increased greatly, connecting Fiji to the world as never before. Within Fiji, the internal transport system improved. A flourishing media — in English as well as Fijian and Hindi — brought the world closer to home. Radio came to many homes in the late 1940s and early 1950s. There was a rapid increase in primary and secondary education. In 1946, there were 438 schools with 36,000 pupils.[30] Ten years later, there were 479 schools with 60,000 pupils. The number of Fijian schools — that is, schools that admitted only Fijian students — increased from 306 in 1946 to 310 in 1955, while the number of Indo-Fijian schools in the same period increased from 106 to 149. Numbers do not, by themselves, reveal the full story. Even though Fijian schools outnumbered Indo-Fijian schools by almost three-to-one, most Fijian schools did not go beyond grade five (only 32 of the 300 schools did), while among Indo-Fijian schools, 84 of the 141 primary schools took their students up to the final year, grade eight. This disparity was evident in other fields as well. In 1958, for instance, there were no professionally qualified Fijian lawyers and only one dentist and one medical doctor. In contrast, there were 38 Indo-Fijian lawyers, 12 medical doctors and eight dentists practising in Fiji. The gap in the educational and professional achievements of the two communities — a result of cultural, historical and economic circumstances — would become a matter of urgent public policy concern for London and Suva in the 1960s.

Three distinct problems faced the new governor, Sir Ronald Garvey, when he assumed office on 6 October 1952: the social and economic problems impeding the progress of the Fijian people, the economic development of the colony in the context of a rising population and limited and ineffectively utilised natural resources, and constitutional reform. Garvey tackled them with the courage and confidence of a man with an intimate acquaintance with islands (he was a close friend of the pre-eminent Fijian leader Ratu Sir Lala Sukuna). He appointed a commission of inquiry, headed by Professor O. H. K. Spate of The Australian National University, to investigate and report on the 'economic activity of Fijian producers, with special attention to the effects of their social organisation on that activity', and to 'consider how far the Fijians' social organisation may be a limited factor in their economic activity, and to suggest in what ways changes in that organisation might be desirable'.[31] Spate's report confirmed the widely held view that Fijians were lagging behind other communities. This was not necessarily because of the success of other groups but because Fijian social institutions and practices, which had evolved in another era and were suited to the needs and requirements of simpler times, had become moribund, smothering the creative life of the community. At the heart of Spate's report was the recommendation to loosen the rigid, stultifying structures of traditional society, to discourage social practices that made unwarranted demands on individual or communal resources and to encourage the gradual growth of individual enterprise and activity among the people — such as *galala* or independent farming — within the overarching ambience of village communities and not as an extraneous, unwelcome extension to them.[32]

To tackle the problem of population growth and economic development, Garvey appointed a commission chaired by Sir Alan Burns and comprising Professor A.

T. Peacock of Edinburgh University and T. Y. Watson, former secretary for agriculture and natural resources in Uganda to 'examine the surveys of the Colony's natural resources and population trends and, having regard to the need to ensure the maintenance of a good standard of living for all sections of the community, to recommend how the development of the Colony and its resources should proceed'.[33] The Burns Commission's recommendations were understandably more far reaching than Spate's. Those of a non-controversial nature — dealing, for instance, with the improvement of local infrastructure and the conditions of agricultural production, extension of the cooperative movement and technical education and the encouragement of independent farming — were accepted by the government and legislation was passed to implement them. The more controversial recommendations, however, especially those dealing with the structure of Fijian society, raised alarm in many Fijian minds.[34] Among the most radical of Burns' proposals was the recommendation to bring the traditional society into the mainstream. Burns recommended the reform and opening up of the separate system of Fijian administration and its replacement with a broad-based multiracial local government.

The separate system of administration, it will be recalled, was established by Sir Arthur Gordon in 1876 as a part of his policy of 'indirect rule', complete with its own secretariat, court system and native regulations designed to 'secure the continuance of the Fijian communal system and the customs and observances traditionally associated with it'.[35] The recommendation to dismantle the administration was opposed by Fijians because they saw their identity and aspirations tied up with it, and because the recommendation came at a time when the political atmosphere in the colony was deeply unsettled. Once emotions had subsided, however, Fijians came around to the view that change was desirable, indeed inevitable, and the system was liberalised substantially in the late 1960s. Among the changes was the abolition of the penal sanctions that had enforced acceptance of subsistence village life for most Fijians and the introduction of elected provincial councils. Fijians were now completely free to remove themselves to towns or other places — as they had already been doing for some time — without having to seek the permission of traditional leaders.

The third problem Garvey tackled was constitutional reform. He informed London that he was convinced of the need for change. 'The position now is that there is a slowly growing interest in constitutional matters, both on the part of the Fijians and the Indians.' Fiji was calm and peaceful, Garvey said, but for how long? 'If we can consider changes in the constitution, now, deliberately and calmly should we not be wise to seize this golden opportunity? There is at present this healthy, if hesitant trend; so should we not seize the growing interest and turn it to our advantage.'[36] Writing to Sir John Macpherson, permanent secretary at the CO, in October 1956, Garvey defended his proposed changes, among which were the removal of official majority from the Legislative Council, the disappearance of nominated members, an increase in the number of Fijian, Indo-Fijian and European members to five (from the existing three), with the Fijian members being elected by the Council of Chiefs itself (rather than the governor selecting names from a list provided by the council) and universal adult franchise for Indo-Fijians and Europeans subject to literary qualification.[37] His most radical proposal — made for the first time — was for the creation of a 'multiracial bench' of four members (one each for the three main racial groups and one for 'other') elected by a weighted common roll.[38] His ultimate goal was a common Fijian citizenship.

> The idea of a multi-racial bench composed of a common vote on a proportional basis, is my own; but I should say here that it has not found much favour with the few official advisers whom I have consulted, though if we are aiming at a growth of a consciousness of Fijian citizenship over-riding differences of race and religion, I think it has considerable merit.[39]

Another of Garvey's controversial proposals was for the abolition of the official majority in the Legislative Council. The main reason — or at least the officially stated reason — for the official majority was to protect special interests, such as the interests of the Fijians and other minorities. In practice, however, Garvey said, he had never found it necessary to use the official majority for that purpose. 'I do not think there is any danger in the Government being defeated if the official majority were removed, always provided the Governor were invested with reserved powers, and I consider that a healthier atmosphere would be created if it went.' Garvey also wanted to abandon the system of nomination. Its abolition would be a popular move, he told London.

> Whatever may be said about nominated members they are always regarded as Government yes-men, even though frequently they are among Government's more trenchant critics, and this taint vitiates them in the public eye. The choice of them becomes more and more difficult, and their value is just as difficult to assess, and little — if anything — would be lost if the system were discontinued.[40]

He was echoing the sentiments of his predecessor, Sir Brian Freeston, who had told London in 1949 that he 'attached little value or importance to maintaining the principle of nominated members, and should shed no tears if the nominated seats ... were thrown open to election'. Garvey also wanted the number of elected European and Indo-Fijian members increased from three to five, and all five Fijian members elected by the Great Council of Chiefs.

On the more controversial of his proposals, Garvey was not supported by his closest senior advisors, who argued that Europeans and Fijians would oppose it, regarding it as the 'thin end of the wedge' leading eventually to common roll, paving the way for reforms too radical for the colony to bear and giving the Indo-Fijian leaders a sense of victory. Some officials were addicted to ingrained habits of thought and were instinctively defensive about any challenge to the underpinnings of their carefully constructed though fragile artefact of the colonial state. There were also many who saw traditional Fijian society — with its well-structured hierarchical system governed by protocol and tradition — through rose-tinted glasses, and who were averse to disturbing its idyllic, unchanging pattern of subsistence life.[41] Garvey remained undaunted, saying that his proposals for encouraging multiracialism were necessary and long overdue if the aim was — as he assumed it to be — the encouragement of a multiracial Fijian citizenship. Preserving the status quo was no solution at all to Fiji's problems.

Nor was Garvey averse to talking bluntly with the Fijian leaders who resisted change. He did this from a position of strength and from strong personal relationships with many leading Fijians, especially Ratu Sir Lala Sukuna. In 1954, Garvey asked the Council of Chiefs to consider directly electing three of their five representatives to the Legislative Council and even floated the idea of adult Fijian franchise. He told the chiefs that the 'chiefly system on which so much depends should march with the times and should not ignore — for too long — the modern trend of democracy'. To those who invoked the Deed of Cession in support of gradualism and permanent paramountcy of Fijian interests, he responded with characteristic though unprecedented bluntness. He addressed the colony in his Cession Day speech in 1957 with a frankness rare in Fiji's history:

> Surely the intention of this Deed, acknowledged and accepted by chiefs who were parties to it, was that Fiji should be developed so as to take a significant place in the affairs of the world but that, in the process, the rights and interests of the Fijian people should be respected. To read into the Deed more than that, to suggest for instance, that the rights and interests of the Fijians should predominate over everything else, does no service either to the Fijian people or their country. The view, for the Fijians, would mean complete protection and no self-respecting individual race wants that because, ultimately, it means that those subject to it will end up as museum pieces. The Indians are equally eligible to have their interests respected. By their work and enterprise, the Indians in Fiji have made a great contribution to the development and prosperity of their country, and to the welfare of its people. They are an essential part of the community and it is unrealistic to suppose that they are not or to imagine the position of Fijians in the world today would benefit by their absence.[42]

Garvey's proposals were discussed widely in the CO, which recommended caution to 'keep a firm grip of the initiative', to act 'just in advance of pressure, but only just'. Any lasting solution to Fiji's problems would have to keep the racial factor firmly in the foreground. Care should be taken not to play into the hands of the Indo-Fijians, which would incite the Fijians, at great cost to the colony. Secretary of State Lloyd wrote to Garvey:

> It seems to us very unwise to do anything to encourage [constitutional reform] to grow more quickly unless we have some fairly clear idea where we are going. In some respects Fiji is a very difficult proposition from the point of view of constitutional advance. We are all, very naturally inclined to think of such advance in terms of British institutions, leading in the direction of an elected assembly, universal adult suffrage, the party system, the vesting of executive power in unofficial Ministers and so forth. Yet we are learning by experience elsewhere that the traditional British pattern, however suitable for places of a certain size, is difficult to work out in small territories, even where there is a homogenous and relatively well advanced population; it is still more difficult to apply in such a place as Fiji, where race means more than party, and where a dilemma is created by the numerical preponderance of the Indo-Fijians on the one hand and our obligation to the Fijians on the other.[43]

In further discussion with Garvey in Suva in June 1957, Philip Rogers, assistant undersecretary of state, shut the door. It was not 'desirable to stimulate constitutional change for its own sake', bearing in mind the 'possibilities of racial conflict' in Fiji.[44] The official majority should be retained, along with nominated members who had an important role to play and who could represent minority communities that sought separate representation, such as Muslims. The spirit of Garvey's multiracial Bench was accepted though not his proposal about how to achieve it. 'We do not care for the system of weighting votes which you propose largely because they would highlight the disparity in size of the electorates and lead to probably irresistible pressure for a, possibly gradual, whittling down of the relative weighting.' By the time a disappointed Garvey left Fiji on 28 October 1958, the need for constitutional reform and change in other areas of the colony's life had been accepted widely. By the late 1950s, the question was its pace and direction.

ENDNOTES

[1] For a succinct summary of early history, see Howe, K. R. 1984, *Where the Waves Fall: A New South Sea Islands History from First Settlement to Colonial Rule*, University of Hawai'i Press, Honolulu. See also Derrick, R. A. 1950, *A History of Fiji*, Government Printer, Suva.

[2] See Routledge, David 1985, *Matanitu: Struggle for Power in Early Fiji*, University of the South Pacific, Suva; and Scarr, Deryck 1973, *The Majesty of Colour. Vol. 1: I, The Very Bayonet*, Australian National University Press, Canberra.

[3] See Legge, J. D. 1958, *Britain in Fiji, 1858–1880*, Macmillan, London.

[4] For an early revisionist account of the Pacific Islands labour trade, which questions this view, see Corris, Peter 1973, *Passage, Port and Plantation: A History of Solomon Islands Labour Migration, 1870–1914*, Melbourne University Press, Melbourne.

[5] See the *Hansard of Legislative Council* debates for this period.

[6] See Tagupa, William E. H. 1991, 'The Unanticipated Republic of Fiji: Deed of Cession as the Constitutional Basis of Legitimacy', in W. Renwick (ed.), *Sovereignty and Indigenous Rights: The Treaty of Waitangi in International Contexts*, Victoria University Press, Wellington, p. 137.

[7] I have been told—but have not been able to verify—that there was a rough translation of the deed in Fijian prepared about the time of cession, but it was never accorded any formal status, and it has never featured in public discourse.

[8] The full text is in Derrick (1950:Appendix [n. 13]).

[9] For a biography of Gordon—somewhat dated now but still the only one available—see Chapman, J. K. 1964, *The Career of Arthur Hamilton Gordon: First Lord Stanmore, 1829–1912*, University of Toronto Press, Toronto.

[10] For a detailed description of the original system of indirect rule, see Legge (1958:[n. 15]).

[11] As pointed out by, among others, Peter France in his remarkable book *The Charter of the Land: Custom and Colonisation in Fiji* (1969, Oxford University Press, Melbourne).

[12] For more on Fijian land tenure and related issues, see Kamikamica, Josefata 1997, 'Fiji native land: issues and challenges', in B. V. Lal and T. R. Vakatora (eds), *Fiji in Transition: Vol. 1 of the Papers of the Fiji Constitution Review Commission*, School of Social and Economic Development, University of the South Pacific, Suva, pp. 259–90.

[13] For a useful survey, see Newbury, Colin 2003, *Patrons, Clients & Empire: Chieftaincy and Over-rule in Asia, Africa, and the Pacific*, Oxford University Press, Oxford, pp. 216–39.

[14] See Moynagh, Michael 1978, 'Brown or White? A History of the Fiji Sugar Industry, 1873–1973', *Pacific Research Monograph Series*, no. 5, The Australian National University, Canberra.

[15] See Gillion, K. L. 1973 (second edn), *Fiji's Indian Migrants: A History to the End of Indenture in 1920*, Oxford University Press, Melbourne; and Lal, Brij V. 1983, 'Girmitiyas: The Origins of the Fiji Indians', *Journal of Pacific History Monograph*, Canberra.

[16] See Gillion (1973:21–2 [n. 27]).

[17] See Lal, Brij V. 1997a, *A Vision for Change: A. D. Patel and the Politics of Fiji*, National Centre for Development Studies, The Australian National University, Canberra, p. 6 (n. 4), quoting the Sanderson Commission (1910): 'The present [Fijian] administration itself fully recognises the value of the Indo-Fijians as permanent settlers and is willing to concede them the enjoyment of equal civil rights. The whole tenor of the correspondence between India and the colony shows that it was on this condition that indentured immigration in Fiji has been allowed in the past, and any measures leading towards lowering the political status of the immigrants or reducing their economic freedom would, in our opinion, involve a breach of faith with those affected.'

[18] An early study of European settlers can be found in Young, John 1984, *Adventurous Spirits: Australian Migrant Society in Pre-Cession Fiji*, University of Queensland Press, St Lucia.

[19] The European community used its position of privilege to attain parity of representation. In turn, this helped consolidate paramountcy by facilitating what later emerged as a de facto alliance of European and Fijian interests to block Indo-Fijian aspirations.

[20] For a succinct survey, see Ali, Ahmed 1980, 'Political Change: From colony to independence', *Plantation to Politics: Studies on Fiji Indians*, University of the South Pacific, Suva, pp. 130–66.

[21] See Gillion, K. L. 1977, *The Fiji Indians: Challenge to European Dominance, 1920–1946*, Australian National University Press, Canberra, pp. 130–56.

22 See Ali (1980:[n. 32]) and Lal, Brij V. 1992, *Broken Waves: A History of the Fiji Islands in the 20th Century*, University of Hawai'i Press, Honolulu, pp. 60–102 (n. 3).

23 Meller, Norman and Anthony, James 1968, *Fiji Goes to the Polls: The Crucial Legislative Council Elections of 1963*, East West Center, Honolulu, p. 16.

24 See Lal (1992:108–58 [n. 3]).

25 A detailed discussion is in Lal, Brij V. 1997b, 'The Decolonisation of Fiji: Debate on Constitutional Change, 1943–1963', in D. Denoon (ed.), *Emerging from Empire? Decolonisation in the Pacific*, Division of Pacific and Asian History, The Australian National University, Canberra, pp. 26–39.

26 Minute by J. B. Sidebottom, 9 September 1947, CO83/245/5.

27 Minute by Sir Charles Jeffries, 18 September 1947, CO83/245/5.

28 In 1956, Fijians numbered 148,134 while Indo-Fijians numbered 169,403 in a total population of 345,737. At the end of 1967, the total population was 502,956, with Fijians making up 41.5 per cent and Indo-Fijians 49.81 per cent.

29 I am indebted to Dr Satya Srivastava for her research on population and Indo-Fijian women in Fiji. See also Chandra, Rajesh and Mason, Keith 1998, *An Atlas of Fiji*, Department of Geography, University of the South Pacific, Suva.

30 These figures are extracted from Fiji *Annual Reports*.

31 Spate, O. H. K 1959, 'The Fijian People: Economic Problems and Prospects', *Legislative Council Paper*, 13/1959.

32 Other academic observers in the 1960s tended to confirm Spate's findings. Among them were: Watters, R. F. 1969, *Koro: Economic Development and Social Change in Fiji*, Oxford University Press, London; and Belshaw, Cyril S. 1964, *Under the Ivi Tree: Society and Economic Growth in Rural Fiji*, Routledge and Kegan Paul, London.

33 Burns, Sir Alan et al. 1960, 'Report of the Commission of Enquiry into the Natural Resources and Population Trends of the Colony of Fiji, 1959', *Legislative Council Paper*, 1/1960.

34 See, for example: Ali, Ahmed 1986, 'Political change, 1874–1960', in B. V. Lal (ed.), *Politics in Fiji: Studies in Contemporary History*, Allen and Unwin, Sydney, pp. 24–5.

35 *Colonial Reports*, 1952, Her Majesty's Stationery Service, Fiji, p. 85.

36 'Constitutional Development', letter from Sir R. Garvey to Sir T. Lloyd, 11 February 1956, CO1036/10, no. 26.

37 Letter from Sir R. Garvey to Sir J. Macpherson, 14 October 1956, CO1036/10, no. 33.

38 For a summary of the correspondence, see 'Constitutional Development B Fiji', 3 October 1958, CO1036/307, no. 18.

39 Letter from Sir R. Garvey to Sir J. Macpherson, 14 October 1956, CO1036/10, no. 3.

40 See Lal (1997b:33 [n. 37]).

41 See, for example, Roth, G. K. 1953, *The Fijian Way of Life*, Oxford University Press, Melbourne.

42 Quoted in Lal (1992:148–9).

43 Lloyd to Garvey, 20 March 1956, CO1036/10, no. 7.

44 P. Rogers to Garvey, 16 January 1957, CO1036/10, no. 36.

3. Amery and the Aftermath

Sir Kenneth Maddocks replaced Garvey in 1958 and remained governor until 1964. Maddocks was different from Garvey in temperament and experience. Born in 1909, he had joined the colonial service in 1929 after graduating from Wadham College, Oxford, and served in Nigeria before coming to Fiji. Unhappily for him, his tenure in Fiji was punctuated by long periods of illness. While he did not have Garvey's sure touch, his familiarity with the Pacific or his wide-ranging friendships across Fiji, Maddocks' Nigerian career provided relevant experience in one important respect. In Northern Nigeria, he had been involved intimately in the process of transforming powerful native authorities into subordinate instruments of local government. Unlike Garvey, however, Maddocks was not one to show vigorous initiative; temperamentally, he was more reactive than proactive.[1] Be that as it may, Maddocks' tenure coincided with perhaps the most turbulent years in Fiji's postwar history. A year after taking office, Maddocks was confronted with deeply damaging industrial unrest in the oil industry in Suva in 1959 and in the sugar industry the next year. The overall effect of the unrest on the governor was to reinforce the importance of caution and gradual change and an acute appreciation of the political realities in the colony.

Maddocks' major concerns throughout his years in office were twofold: to address the imbalance between the two main races in the public service and to forge an appropriate path for the orderly constitutional development of the colony. Fijians were not only under-represented in the professions, as we have already seen; they were greatly outnumbered in the higher echelons of the civil service. This under-representation had a number of causes. Among them was the reluctance of traditional leaders, including Ratu Sukuna, to encourage academic education for their people whose appropriate place, they felt, was in the villages.[2] Indeed, a revamped Fijian Administration in 1944 had strengthened the authority of the traditional structures of Fijian society, especially the power of chiefs. While Fijians were advised to stay close to their traditional cultural roots under the guidance of their chiefs, Indo-Fijians were actively pursuing higher education for their children attending community-funded schools. The gap presented the officials with a delicate and difficult situation when making civil service appointments: preserving the principle of merit on the one hand, and increasing Fijian presence on the other.

To improve Fijian prospects in the civil service, separate scholarships under the Colonial Welfare and Development Scheme were inaugurated to enable select individuals to receive special training in the United Kingdom. Interestingly, the scheme did not attract much adverse comment from the Indo-Fijian community, which was excluded from it, partly because its leaders had a prudent appreciation of its importance for the overall development of Fiji. During the 1960s, the special training schemes did increase, if not dramatically, the number of Fijians in the civil service. There were other unexpected benefits as well. The elite of the emerging Fijian leadership on scholarship in the United Kingdom came in contact and socialised with officials in places that mattered. Through informal and personal contacts, officials in London gained deeper and more sympathetic insights into Fijian thinking on critical issues, while a period in the United Kingdom increased Fijians' already considerable respect and affection for English institutions and values. The Indo-Fijian leaders had no such opportunity and no such contacts.

On the constitutional front, Maddocks sought advice from the CO about electoral systems and constitutional arrangements in other places that might have some relevance for Fiji. In particular, he inquired about the so-called 'Tanganyika Model' and about the functioning of legislative councils with unofficial majorities.[3] The Tanganyika Model provided a mix of communal as well as common-roll seats, the latter reserved for each of the three principal racial groups of Europeans, Africans and Asians. Regarding the Tanganyika Model, the CO replied that the

> crux of the matter is whether representation is to be on a racial or a party basis. If the intention is that the Fijians, Indians and Europeans should have the opportunity to return candidates acceptable to the majority of their respective *races*, thereby perpetuating communal divisions, then the Tanganyika system does not appear to be the solution.[4]

It would work to produce inter-racial cooperation if politics were conducted on party lines.

It was, however, the Tanganyika Model that was adopted in Fiji, where political participation had always been racially compartmentalised and where political parties were only recently formed — the Federation Party in 1963 and the Alliance Party in 1966, just a year before the introduction of a new electoral system. As for an unofficial majority, the CO advised against it. The practice had been used in a number of places — in Aden, Gibraltar, Tanganyika, Uganda and elsewhere — but the experience 'tended to produce frustration and to strengthen premature unofficial demands for greater executive representation and authority'.[5] Official majority in Fiji's Legislative Council was not removed until after a constitutional conference in 1965.

Fiji's unique set-up required careful deliberation. Given the colony's history and ethnic sensitivities, the CO conceded that representation would have to continue on racial lines, but it did not favour extension on a racial basis. 'We think the important thing is to keep the way open for the development of non-racialism in Fiji politics and not to take any avoidable action which involves establishing or confirming institutional forms embodying racial divisions,' wrote P. Rogers to the governor. 'We should, on the contrary, seek constantly to edge the community in the way of non-racial attitudes and behaviour, political and social, and to afford it time to develop and adopt such attitudes and behaviour.'[6] As far as constitutional change was concerned, 'we want to keep one pace, but not two paces, in front of real political feeling and we certainly want to avoid widespread feelings of frustration'. The CO advised the governor to hold consultation with his senior officials and present fresh proposals for constitutional advance.

This the governor had been doing in any case with his most senior advisors: P. D. Macdonald, the colonial secretary, and Q. V. L. Weston, the assistant colonial secretary, with long experience of Fiji, the latter since 1940.[7] Their views differed considerably. Weston argued that the only way Fijians could be persuaded to accept constitutional reform was if the paramountcy of their interests was acknowledged explicitly, perhaps through extra seats in the legislature. He cited the Deed of Cession in justification. Fijians were the indigenous community, they owned more than 80 per cent of the land and had always been loyal to the Crown. The reference to loyalty was intended to remind London of the Fijian's distinguished record of service in World War II. This contrasted markedly with the record of the Indo-Fijians, who largely abstained from service during the war — partly in protest against the racially discriminatory rates of pay soldiers received, and partly because the government distrusted their loyalty and wanted them to contribute to the war effort by remaining on their farms.[8] Once the principle of paramountcy was accepted, Weston argued, the way would open for the introduction of a limited number of common-roll seats on the Tanganyika Model. The Indo-Fijian community, he thought, could be placated by reducing the number of European seats in the Legislative Council. He proposed doubling the number of Fijian members relative to the number of Indo-Fijian members (from five to 10), with the additional five being nominated by the Council of Chiefs.

Macdonald, with whose views Maddocks eventually agreed, opted for the retention of racial voting and the principle of parity. Common roll, in any shape or form, was anathema to Fijians and Europeans, he argued, and it would be impossible to gain their acquiescence to its introduction. For their part, Indo-Fijians could not be expected to accept Fijian paramountcy without protest, nor would Europeans be likely to accept reduction in their own numbers. European representation in its present form was necessary 'both in order to protect the Fijian, and in order to ensure that the confidence of European businessmen and investors in Fiji, now already shaken, does not result in a flight of capital and cessation of investment'. The way forward, Macdonald advised, was to reduce official numbers in the Legislative Council — something that had been opposed by Suva and London in the past — and introduce a 'member' system in which unofficial members were given supervisory roles over collections of government departments.

These views were being canvassed in Suva when parliamentary undersecretary of state at the CO, Julian Amery, arrived in Fiji. Amery was a well-connected Conservative (his father, Leopold, had been secretary of state for India in the 1940s), supremely self-confident and had a penchant for sharp, unequivocal judgments. During his two years (1958–60) at the CO, he developed a particular interest in island colonies, whether in the Caribbean, Mediterranean or the Pacific. While his views did not always command support among officials, they always demanded attention. Amery arrived in Fiji at a particularly unfortunate time, when the colony was in the middle of a prolonged and devastating strike in the sugar industry. Some Indo-Fijian leaders, including A. D. Patel, told their followers that Amery had been sent by London to help end the strike. That, of course, was not strictly the case, though the purpose of the visit was deliberately cloaked in secrecy and thus open to all sorts of interpretation. Feelings were inflamed against the Indo-Fijians, with troops being sent to the sugar belts to 'protect' farmers who wanted to harvest. Fijians were still reeling from the recommendations of the Spate and Burns commissions, feeling isolated, apprehensive and abandoned. Understandably, their attitude to change had hardened.

The timing of Amery's visit was critical because his recommendations were to have a far-reaching effect on thinking about official policy towards Fiji (his report is reproduced in Appendix 1).[9] The problem of the racial divide was already known in London, and the CO had access to a wide range of informed opinion about the colony. Amery, however, put the issue vividly so that his name and words echoed in most major policy statements throughout the 1960s. He was blunt in his assessment. 'The Fijians and Indians are more distinct as communities than Jews and Arabs in Palestine, Greeks and Turks in Cyprus or even Europeans and Bantu in South and Central Africa.'[10] Fijians feared Indian domination, and had hardened their attitude to change. Their confidence in British intentions had been shaken. They regarded the recommendations of the Burns Commission for internal reform within Fijian society 'as an attempt to give the Indian community control of the land by breaking up traditional Fijian society'. It had to be remembered that it was the Fijians who had been the loyal community — the reference here being to the non-active participation of the Indo-Fijian community in the war effort. The Fijians provided 75 per cent of the armed forces. 'The islands could hardly be governed without them, let alone against them.' This was an obvious point, but it had not been made by a responsible official in such stark terms before. Amery continued:

> We must, I think, accept that it is impracticable to think in terms of a single Fijian nation or of a common roll at any rate for the foreseeable future. Any suggestion of this is bound to arouse Fijian suspicions that the Indian would dominate by counting heads. The moderate Indo-Fijian leaders recognise this. This points to the conclusion that we shall have to recognise the equality of the Indian and Fijian communities irrespective of their numbers. There is no other way of reconciling both the pledges in the Deed of Cession and those in Lord Salisbury's despatch, let alone the need to keep communal peace. We should, therefore, let it be known that any constitutional advance must be so designed as to preclude the domination of one of the two main communities by the other.

Instead of gradually abolishing the separate system of Fijian Administration, as the Burns Commission had recommended, Amery urged its retention because the Fijians were 'determined to resist any move in this direction'. Indeed, he recommended an Indian counterpart to it. The principle of parity in the civil service — in each grade of each department — should be the aim of the government. Finally, Amery recommended a move towards a 'quasi-ministerial system' while retaining the official majority in the Legislative Council. His overall policy direction was clear.

> Hitherto we have held up the concept of a single multi-racial community as the goal towards which Fijians and Indians alike should strive. The Fijians will no longer accept this; and the more we lay the emphasis on multi-racialism, the more suspicious they will become that we plan to sell them out to the Indo-Fijians. The only way, in my view, to exorcise the fear of communal domination, is to make it clear — as of now — that we stand for equal rights for both communities and that we shall not pull out until both ask us to do so.

Amery's views were canvassed widely in the CO. It was generally agreed that Amery's prognosis was probably correct, though some remarked on the unfortunate timing of the visit, with industrial riots in Suva in December 1959 and the strike in the sugar industry in 1960. The latter was regarded by the Fijians 'as an Indian attempt to gain control of the sugar industry which is vital to Fiji's economy. These fears of the Indians have consolidated the Fijian ranks and made them most reluctant to give any concessions which they think would be to the advantage of the Indians.'[11] Sir Hilton Poynton, the permanent undersecretary, accepted that the challenge of making Fiji into a cohesive non-racial state was difficult, but argued that 'to decide now that we should abandon the attempt [towards non-racialism] and base all our future policy on a constitutional and racial partition (even though not a geographical one) seems to me to be a counsel of despair'.[12] If Amery's view were accepted, Poynton went on:

We should be left perpetually holding the ring between what in effect amounted to two separate administrations and communities in Fiji. This might be all right for a time and might get us out of some immediate political difficulties. But the time is bound to come when there is a demand for at least full internal self-government in Fiji and possibly even national independence — especially when New Zealand grants Western Samoa independence next year. I should hate to find ourselves in the kind of position that we faced in Palestine between Jews and Arabs or in Cyprus between Greeks and Turks with the racial antagonism aggravated and, indeed, officially recognised in the constitution and ourselves unable to let go without leaving Civil War in our trail when we went. To abandon our policies for such a counsel of despair is a very big decision to take before we reverse the engines. If we do reverse them I doubt we would ever be able to re-reverse them again. The specific recommendation with parity in the Legislative Council or in the Executive Council or in the public service, and the question of whether or not to abolish the Fijian Administration are really subsidiary to this major issue of long term policy.

Elsewhere in the CO, there was general consensus on the broad thrust of Amery's report. The strength of the Fijian opposition had to be recognised and respected. The Fijian Administration would not be abolished in favour of a more multiracial system of local government. After all, the Fijian government, with CO authorisation, had done much in the 1940s to reinvigorate the separate system of Fijian administration, elevating 'chiefs to greater status and authority than they had ever held before',[13] partly as reward for the enthusiastic Fijian war effort and partly because of the enormous influence of the pre-eminent Fijian chief, Oxford-educated and decorated soldier Ratu Sir Lala Sukuna, the traditionalist panjandrum of impeccable conservative credentials, who was also Secretary for Native Affairs.[14] Fijians had their reasons for refusing to accept change, but London was also caught in a bind: it could not reverse the wheels it had set in motion and reject the legitimacy and foundations of an order it had nurtured so assiduously. Robert Norton has remarked on the irony of the CO's position: approving 'the reinforcement of chiefly power and ethnic separation just as it was embark[ing] on the project of decolonisation throughout the empire'. This contradiction, he continues, 'encouraged the reactionary stance of the newly empowered Fijian elite: their determination well into the 1960s, to cling defensively to colonial rule as the rulers prepared to end it'.[15]

Some of Amery's other recommendations were rejected. The idea of a separate Indian administration was not only unacceptable in principle because of London's long-term commitment to multiracialism, it was impracticable because of the structure and settlement pattern of the Indo-Fijian community. Fijians needed help and protection, officials in London agreed, but they had also to be taught 'to face up to modern economic realities' — and officials favoured the gradual racial integration of public institutions. Amery's offhand remark that women should not be enfranchised if men did not favour it was shrugged off as an itinerant thought of an idiosyncratic mind. In November, Poynton wrote to Maddocks that Amery's recommendation to retain the communal system was 'purely a continuation of the present set-up, and [the governor was] not to be drawn into any statement that this is to be the pattern for all time'. The long-term goal was a non-racial state. This was to be achieved through a 'withering away' rather than 'an overt extinction of the communal roots of society'. He emphasised also to the governor that 'we should avoid any statement which commits us forever to communal representation'.[16] The overall impact in London of Amery's visit was summarised by Hugh Fraser, Amery's successor as parliamentary undersecretary of state. He described the CO's stand as a holding position or middle course between 'the Burns non-racial line and the Amery communal approach'. Fiji was a potential trouble spot in the Pacific. Sooner or later (the next year, according to Fraser), clearer policy guidelines would be needed.[17]

On the future of the Fijian Administration, about which Amery had expressed firm views, Poynton said that the CO accepted that its abolition in the present circumstances was 'just not on', though he hoped that 'something should be done to streamline and modernise it insofar it affects the development of individualism amongst the Fijians'. In particular, he encouraged the governor to encourage *galala* (independent) farming. 'We think that an increase in the number of *galala* would encourage enlightened self-interest amongst the Fijians and probably bring them into greater contact with the realities of life and possibly also with Indians and Europeans. This, in due course, should have some effect on their political outlook.'[18] Encouragement did not, however, come from where it mattered most: from the leading chiefs in the provinces, who feared the corrosive impact of *galala* on their leadership and the overall cohesion of indigenous village community, and from the officials of the Fijian Administration, who were opposed to it from the start — opposed to the 'withering away' of their cherished handiwork.

While waiting for a fuller policy on constitutional advance, Maddocks sought the CO's approval of the Fijian government's draft proposal for constitutional reform. The reform was to proceed in two stages. In the first stage, selected unofficial members of the Legislative Council would be invited to accept supervisory roles — with no executive authority — over a number of government departments, working within the conventional framework of collective responsibility exercised in the Executive Council: the membership system. The second stage would be a transition to a full ministerial system in which members would exercise executive responsibility. London approved the governor's proposal, with the proviso that the title 'member' would be used in the first stage and 'minister' with full executive authority in the second — much to the disappointment of Maddocks, who thought the term 'member' was a colourless one while the use of 'minister 'might make it more acceptable and also inculcate a greater sense of responsibility'. But he 'would not stand on this point'.[19]

The government's constitutional proposals were debated in the Legislative Council between 21 and 24 April 1961. It was the liveliest debate for years. What mattered more than anything else was the reaction of the Fijian leaders. With one lone exception (Semesa Sikivou), all of them rejected the motion, which, the government was at pains to explain, was not seeking approval or decision but was intended to gauge the views of the people. E. R. Bevington, the Acting Colonial Secretary, said in an almost pleading tone: '

> We have had our constitution for a long time. We must look into the future and try to establish for ourselves a long term objective. If we don't, we will lack a sense of direction. It is not good sitting down and saying 'I want the status quo.' Changes are taking place and we must decide how we are going to move with these events. We don't want to wait until these forces have built up against us and we have to do things as a matter of urgency. Let us think ahead. Let us see what is coming. Let us be ready for it and let us do what we have got to do in our own time and by our own choosing. Do not let us forget the forces outside. They are there and they are real.[20]

Ratu Mara, who by a combination of his intellect, education and chiefly birth had emerged as the dominant Fijian leader by the early 1960s,[21] set the mood. Confident that he was speaking for the majority of the Fijian people, he opposed the motion. 'The reason why I am opposed to this motion is that I feel the direction is towards the complete independence of the Colony even though it might be in the Commonwealth.' The proposals were 'ill-conceived' and 'ill-timed', Ratu Mara said, accusing the government of ignoring the Deed of Cession, which, he suggested, had never contemplated the severance of the link between Fiji and the United Kingdom.[22] In private, however, he tended to be less dogmatic. Fijians, he said, would accept constitutional reform towards greater self-government if Fiji were guaranteed a continuing link to the United Kingdom similar to that enjoyed by the Channel Islands and the Isle of Man. This was the first mention in Fiji of a proposal often mooted publicly subsequently that Fiji might somehow be integrated with the United Kingdom.

Ratu Penaia Ganilau, an important conservative Fijian leader close to his people, supporting Mara, chided the government for not consulting the public before announcing the constitutional proposals and raised fears about the introduction of common roll. Ravuama Vunivalu, perhaps the ablest debater on the Fijian side, summed up what he called the message from the Fijian people. 'We cannot reconcile the implications of these proposals with the assurances that have been given from time to time that our interests in this, our native land, shall always remain paramount.' His people regarded the Deed of Cession as 'a contract which can only be revoked by mutual agreement of the two contracting parties. There can be no question of a unilateral revocation.' In any future constitutional arrangements, he continued, Fijians must have majority representation in the Executive as well as the Legislative Councils. He also asked the government for an 'unequivocal statement' about its 'interpretation of the place of Deed of Cession in the affairs of this colony today'. Fijian preconditions for accepting constitutional reform were made explicit for the first time: recognition of the principle of paramountcy of Fijian interests and a continuing link with the United Kingdom. Nothing less was acceptable.

The Fijians' united opposition to the proposals for constitutional reform had its effect on the government. In July 1961, the governor sought clearance from the CO for a passage he intended to include in his Cession Day address in October to reassure the Fijian people that the pace of change towards internal self-government would heed the advice of their leaders. Maddocks wanted London to agree that it would not 'hand over power until a substantial measure of agreement has been reached among the different races'. and that before the introduction of self-government, 'agreement would have to be reached about the safeguarding of legitimate Fijian interests after the transfer of power'.[23]

The first condition was superfluous: Fijians could not be forced into self-government against their wish, H. P. Hall minuted. At the same time, the United Kingdom could 'not accept a Fijian veto on any changes whatsoever [for example] the introduction of the membership system'. Sir H. Poynton was characteristically blunter:

> The doctrine of consent is an admirable one if you can get consent; but if you cannot then the Secretary of State cannot escape the responsibility for taking a decision. To give one community in a colony a power of veto over constitutional changes even when that community is the indigenous race in a multi-racial community, is tantamount to an abdication by the Secretary of State of his responsibilities to Parliament for the orderly constitutional development of the territory. The point of principle is the same whether we are talking about the Fijians in Fiji, the Dominion Party in Rhodesia or the late Group Captain Briggs in Kenya.[24]

The CO view prevailed. London had 'no intention of forcing the pace of constitutional advance in Fiji', it advised the governor, by declaring that the 'extent and timing of such advance will continue to take into account the need to safeguard legitimate Fijian interests and [Her Majesty's Government] will only decide on any major changes after full consultation with the representatives of the various communities in the colony'. Notwithstanding Fijian opposition, it was 'in the general interest that some measure of increased responsibility should be given to unofficial members as soon as they are ready'.[25] The concept of a Fijian veto was removed. Maddocks had also flagged the subject of increased Fijian numbers in the Legislative Council to recognise the principle of Fijian paramountcy.[26] He suggested six Fijian members — four elected and two nominated by the Council of Chiefs — and five Indo-Fijian and European members each, four elected and one nominated.

London required a fuller explanation for a proposal that entailed a fundamental redirection of policy, upsetting the principle of parity that had been the hallmark of Fiji's constitutional arrangements since 1937. In a long dispatch of 21 July 1961, the Acting Governor, P. D. Macdonald, provided the justification.[27] An extra seat for Fijians, Macdonald argued, would among other things be a 'token of positive recognition by Her Majesty's Government of the rights of the Fijians in their own country, and also of their loyal, spontaneously offered, and meritorious services in two World Wars and in the emergency in Malaya, in which conflicts Indians in Fiji contributed virtually nothing'. An additional seat might encourage the Fijians to move forward towards a membership or ministerial system more readily and even encourage them to have a more liberal attitude towards the vexed land issue. For Fijians, Macdonald continued, land was the issue at the heart of the debate. 'They have, as you will be aware, a deep-seated and by no means unreasonable fear that the Legislature will one day come under the control of the Indians, who will amend legislation in such a way as to remove from the Fijians, not only the control over, but also the title to, their lands,' he wrote. Fijian loyalty was

> closely related to the undertakings concerning their land which they read into the Deed of Cession and it seems certain at present that there will be no further measure of constitutional advance in the foreseeable future unless firm safeguards are written either into any future constitution or proclaimed in some other way as to ensure that the title to their lands cannot be taken from them.

Macdonald was rehearsing well-known prejudices and fears that had long informed colonial politics. There was no conceivable way that Indo-Fijians, or anyone else for that matter, including the colonial government itself, could dispossess Fijians of their lands and other assets. Europeans had tried to do this and failed in the early years of the twentieth century. The enormous practical difficulties aside — the Fijians, after all, dominated the armed forces, as Amery had so clearly stated — Indo-Fijian leaders had repeatedly stated since the 1940s that the ownership of land was not at issue; the terms and conditions on which it was leased were. This was the view of the colonial government itself. The Burns Commission had made the same point in its wide-ranging report. Macdonald knew, however, even as he wrote to London, that his claim about the Indo-Fijian 'take over bid for Fiji', as he put it, lacked substance and conviction. If Fijians could not be given an additional seat, he would be content with the principle of parity.

The CO rejected the proposal for an additional Fijian member for the Legislative Council. A. R. Thomas, assistant undersecretary of state, noted that this 'would be needlessly provocative to Indians faced with opposition to have anything short of parity of representation between them'.[28] Maddocks conceded that giving Fijians one more seat was not the best way of protecting Fijian interests; it was the governor's duty to protect the vital interests of the people, especially the Fijian people.[29] London also rejected the proposal that the unofficial members of the Executive Council should be elected by the Legislative Council as a whole, preferring them to be appointed at the governor's discretion. The principle of electing unofficial members could complicate the appointment of a chief minister when the full ministerial system came in. It would be best to let the governor appoint the person best able to command majority support in the lower house. Alsp, common roll, even in a limited form, was 'clearly unacceptable at present because of the attitude of the Fijians and the Europeans'.[30] The best that could be hoped for was a 'bridge' between common roll and communal roll.

Fijian concerns and interests and how best to accommodate them did not fade away. The next year, 1962, Maddocks resumed his correspondence on the subject, reminding London of the difficulty he encountered in getting the Fijians to accept the idea of inter-racial local government.[31] This had been one of the recommendations of the Burns Commission. 'The insurmountable obstacle to the introduction of local government,' he told the CO,

> is the fear of the Fijians that any advance towards inter-racialism in matters of importance is a step towards Indian domination. The Fijians judge this proposal, as they did proposals for an extension of inter-racial education, the abolition of the Fijian Administration, and constitutional reform, not on logical or utilitarian grounds, but from the point of view of the effect which such proposals will have on the status of the Fijians in relation to the Indo-Fijians. Any reform or innovation calculated in their opinion to undermine the racial identity of the Fijians is condemned irrespective of its merits, and any significant development towards inter-racialism is liable to be regarded by the Fijians as having this tendency.

He quoted the words of Ratu Penaia Ganilau and Ratu George Cakobau during the 1961 Legislative Council debate that at independence Fiji should be handed back to the Fijians. This sentiment, he said, was shared broadly by many in the indigenous community. The reference to Amery's report in the dispatch gave an insight into the governor's broad frame of mind and that of his senior officers, many of whom supported the principle of Fijian paramountcy in any case. This concession, they felt, was necessary to get the Fijians to accept change. The best way forward, Maddocks suggested, was 'Fijian racial majority on the Legislative and Executive Councils, with the Indo-Fijians next in numbers, and the Europeans combined with the other racial groups, coming last'.

The reply from the CO was blunt and was informed by growing anti-colonial pressure at the United Nations and by studies undertaken by the CO itself of Fiji's place in the wider context of U policy towards its remaining colonial dependencies. The Fijians could not expect the United Kingdom to be in control of Fiji in perpetuity. Nor could London accept the recognition of Fijian paramountcy as practicable. It would find it difficult persuading the Indo-Fijian community to accept the principle when it constituted the majority population. Secretary of State, Duncan Sandys, told Maddocks:

> I do not see that we could possibly persuade, and it would be wrong and impossible politically to try to compel, the Indians to accept a constitution which recognized Fijian paramountcy. Ever were we to do so and however such a provision was entrenched. I find it unrealistic to think that they, with a growing majority of the population, their economic dominance and well known propensity for self-advancement, would accept it after our departure, and I should expect them to receive considerable outside support in revolting against what would surely seem to the world at large to be the negation of democracy. However innocent the Fijians may be of the historical developments which have brought the Indians to the position today. The Indians are there to stay and their position must inevitably become increasingly important. It seems to me that any solution which does not recognize these facts is doomed to fail.[32]

Sandys then suggested another approach, a kind of 'shock tactic' — that is, to tell Fijians that they could not expect the United Kingdom to hold their privileged position indefinitely, and that the 'only future for Fiji worthy of her past and suitable for her position in the modern world is as a multiracial state in which citizens of all races have full opportunity to play their part according to their abilities'. Multiracialism was not only a desirable goal but an attainable one, Sandys continued. To 'fall back either on entrenched separation or on the indefinite continuation of the *status quo* is a counsel of despair'. He sought further 'positive recommendations' from Maddocks about the future direction of constitutional policy.

Sandys' dispatch was a document of uncommon candour, intentionally, provocatively designed to force Suva to fresh, creative thinking about alternative solutions to Fiji's complicated problems. It was sent when the CO was also contemplating what to say about Fiji in preparation for regional talks at the official level in Washington on the future of colonial territories in the Pacific with representatives from the US, Australian and New Zealand governments. A draft on Fiji was described by officials as controversial, because it tried to outline 'the makings of a policy for resolving the Colony's internal problems which we frankly have not yet got'.[33] Three solutions were under consideration — abandoning attempts to foster integration, acknowledging Fijian paramountcy or furthering attempts to bring the communities together — but the United Kingdom had yet to decide which to pursue. Only one point seemed certain: the economic value of Fiji to Britain was described as 'nil'.

To the extent that Sandys' dispatch was designed to provoke a response, Maddocks rose to the challenge. The governor stood his ground and responded equally forthrightly.[34] The policy of nudging Fiji towards multiracialism would contradict past assurances given to Fijians about their special place in the country, he said, and would provoke 'anger and amazement' among them — and Europeans and Fijians would feel betrayed. The policy of multiracialism 'would destroy the balance between the races which rests on the Fijians being accorded protection for which, in return, they have given their full cooperation to government, and have adopted a tolerant attitude towards the Indians'. Echoing Amery, Maddocks continued that if Fijians lost confidence in the British, they might embark on the path of passive resistance, which would hinder moves towards self-government and might even lead to violence. London, he said, did not appreciate fully the strength of the Fijian opposition to change. Nor did it appreciate that not all Indo-Fijians wanted multiracial self-government; many had a prudent and pragmatic appreciation of the Fijian position. Of course, Britain could not be expected to hold on to Fiji indefinitely, but it was too soon to announce that policy publicly. Nor was it wise of London to be preoccupied with long-term goals. The best way forward was to prepare the ground for internal self-government, and acknowledge the special position of the Fijians, perhaps through a Treaty of Friendship similar to the one enjoyed by Tonga.

Maddocks acknowledged the deleterious effects of a racially segregated electoral system, but was also mindful of total Fijian and European opposition to non-racial politics. This problem could be solved partly through the adoption of the Tanganyika Model. The Fijian people were not unreasonable, Maddocks assured the CO; they would accept change if they felt their vital interests were protected. He continued:

> The type of compromise solution that I have in mind, and to which the Indians might well agree, is that when, ultimately, Fiji reaches the stage at which it is appropriate to appoint a chief minister, the chief minister should be a Fijian; that legislation affecting rights over Fijian land should require a majority of two-thirds or three-quarters of those present and voting; and that a balance in the Civil Service should be preserved. This would be a departure from the usual practice but no more so than was

approved in the case of the constitution of Malaya; but if anything is certain it is that the normal democratic practices of the western world will not, in the foreseeable future, work here.

Within Fiji, with elections due in early 1963 and with the announcement of Undersecretary of State Nigel Fisher's visit about that time, the leaders began to manoeuvre for advantage. Among them was Ratu Mara. Although sometimes voicing liberal opinion in private, he adopted a hardline approach in public. For example, he acknowledged privately that the system of Fijian administration was in need of an overhaul. He favoured the introduction of multiracial local government, and the introduction of the membership system; but he opposed them in public for fear of alienating his Fijian constituency. In a private meeting with other high chiefs in September 1962, Mara alleged that while in London, he had sighted an agreement between Ratu Sukuna and the British government on the future of the Fijian people, implying that London was reneging on the agreement. '*Me satini vakavinaka mada na nomu masi*', the Fiji Special Branch reported him as saying, 'Be prepared to go to war or be prepared to accept whatever is given to you.'[35] No one in the CO knew anything about the supposed secret agreement, while Sir Ronald Garvey said 'with absolute certainty, so far as I am concerned, that no such document exists'.[36] It was in all probability a political ploy to put pressure on the government about the protection of Fijian interests. Mara perplexed officials in London. '[H]aving preached to all of us while he was here the need for Fijians to emerge into the modern world,' wrote J. E. Marnham to Garvey, '[he] has since his return been playing the arch-traditionalist guardian of every jot and title of Fijians rights.'[37] Garvey thought the emerging Fijian leader 'very intelligent with a weird dose of immaturity mixed up with it and extremely ambitious both for himself and his people'.[38]

At the same time, the CO grappled with Maddocks' suggestion about the Tanganyika Model: it was relevant and appropriate superficially, but problematic on closer scrutiny.[39] The governor wanted a predetermined outcome: Fijians on top, with a Fijian chief minister. An appropriate — not necessarily a democratic — system would have to be devised to achieve that outcome. There were other problems as well. The Tanganyika Model worked well because political parties existed in that country. There were no political parties in Fiji when the governor advanced the proposal. Moreover, the population was unevenly distributed racially throughout the colony, which, as one CO official commented, would make it silly to have a constituency dominated by Indo-Fijians, with few Fijians and hardly any Europeans, and yet have a seat each for the three races.[40] In the end, Maddocks' view about constitutional advancement prevailed, with London proposing to reassure the governor that in future, a 'more gradual programme' of change would be adopted.[41]

Simultaneously, questions were asked about whether anything was to be learned by comparing the position of Indo-Fijians in Fiji with that of the Chinese in Malaya. Not much, it was found: the historical and contemporary situations of the two communities were different.[42]

Nigel Fisher, parliamentary undersecretary for the colonies, visited Fiji in January 1963 as part of his wider Pacific tour, the purpose being 'to listen, to confirm a view, and to advise the Secretary of State on his return'.[43] He was advised to use 'verbal ingenuity' to avoid causing 'alarm and despondency' by suggesting that the United Kingdom was about to force constitutional change upon the people of Fiji, but at the same time 'avoid saying anything which might be interpreted as a pledge not to introduce change until all sections of the community wanted it'. Fisher proved equal to the task. In Fiji, he listened carefully to a wide range of opinion through petitions and submissions. H. G. Nicholls, chief inspector of the CSR in Fiji, urged London not to 'turn Fiji loose as a self governing territory without ensuring that it can depend in many essential ways on the neighbouring and friendly countries who are more advanced and economically stronger'.[44] The Suva Chamber of Commerce expressed the fear that 'if the British administration in the Colony ceases, our rights as free citizens of a democratic state may be seriously affected', and it urged Britain to safeguard their economic interests as traders and their citizenship rights, promote more local government and adopt a policy of gradual localisation.[45]

London wanted above all to gauge the breadth and depth of Fijian opinion about the pace and direction of constitutional change, for as the correspondence from Amery onwards shows, it was what the Fijians thought that counted. What it heard was sobering. The Fijian Cane Growers Industrial Congress, based in western Viti Levu, the heartland of Indo-Fijian settlement, bluntly said: 'We Fijians will not give up our rights. We would like to state that there should be no changes in the present constitution of the colony until [the] Council of Chiefs and we Fijian people express our desire for further Constitutional changes.' They wanted to be reassured that the bond between the Fijian people and the Crown was intact. 'We [would] very much like to know whether our bond with [the] Crown [is] still the same as when our Fijian Chiefs ceded our land and people to Queen Victoria.'[46] Apisai Tora, a politician and trade unionist, made a written submission in which he railed against the Indo-Fijians, the government and Fijian chiefs, demanding more representative administration and more representation of Fijians in it.[47]

Tora could be — and was — dismissed, but not so the Fijian Affairs Board. Its submission — popularly known as the 'Wakaya Letter' after the Fijian island on which it was formulated — captured the various strands of Fijian political thinking and articulated them with force and coherence for the first time.[48] The letter was signed by all members of the Fijian Affairs Board, which consisted of three 'paramount' chiefs with the highest ranks in Fiji: Ratu Mara (from Lau), Ratu Penaia Ganilau (Cakaudrove) and Ratu George Cakobau (Bau). Its other signatories were A. C. Reid and R. M. Major, both senior civil servants, and J. N. Falvey, European member of the Legislative Council and the board's legal advisor. The letter asked for the 'spirit and substance' of the Deed of Cession to be strengthened, links between Fiji and the United Kingdom preserved — along the lines enjoyed by the Channel Islands and the Isle of Man — Fijian land rights secured, Fiji to be declared a Christian state and the policy of racial parity in the civil service enforced. Only then would Fijians entertain the possibility of further constitutional change. The letter reminded the CO of the 'insistence of the Fijian people that the initiative for any constitutional change should come from them'. The Wakaya Letter, with its demand for Fijian veto power on matters of constitutional change, was a powerful negotiating document with wide-ranging implications. Its existence became known publicly in January 1963 — long after it was first presented.

Nigel Fisher reassured the Fijians that the United Kingdom would respect the terms of the Deed of Cession, although he pointed out accurately enough that the deed was 'primarily concerned with the transfer of sovereignty over Fiji to Her Majesty's Government'.[49] He undertook to examine the proposal for Fiji to have a relationship similar to that the United Kingdom enjoyed with the Channel Islands. He reassured the Indo-Fijian community that they were equal, not second-class, citizens of Fiji. And he emphasised the need to develop a more multiracial approach to the problems facing Fiji. Sandys wrote to the governor in August 1963 to say that he had 'studied carefully' the contents of the Wakaya Letter. He hoped for further progress towards internal self-government but 'in consultation with representatives of the people of Fiji', and not one section of it as demanded by the Fijians.[50] As for a relationship along the lines of the Channel Islands, the circumstances of the two countries were dissimilar, so the constitutional arrangements would be different although where appropriate some relevant features might be adapted for Fiji. Opinion within Whitehall was rather more candid on this point. In a note for an Official Committee on Future Policy in the Pacific in April 1963, the CO weighed the arguments for and against the United Kingdom confirming that a link of some sort would be maintained between Fiji and Britain.[51] On balance, the arguments were in favour, despite the difficulties this might cause with the anti-colonial movement at the United Natioms and the precedent that might be seized on by other UK territories anxious for similar treatment. Confirmation of a continuing link — its precise form to be determined later — was required to persuade the Fijians to enter a constitutional dialogue and, while other colonial powers would have to be consulted, a continuing link would doubtless please the Americans for whom strategic considerations were uppermost in deciding whether Pacific territories might progress to independence. The United Kingdom agreed that the 'creation of new independent states should be undertaken only if adequate arrangements for the security of the area involved can be assured'.[52] The Foreign Office in Whitehall was never backward in reminding the CO of the importance of the strategic dimension.

Against this background Sandys proposed in August 1963 a constitutional conference in London to 'try and agree upon concrete proposals' for constitutional change.[53] In April 1964, the CO gave the new governor, Sir Derek Jakeway, who had assumed office in January, its response to the Wakaya Letter and outlined broadly the line he might take in his discussions with the leaders in Fiji. London would try to work out a constitution that was as advanced 'as the Fijians will swallow'. The links with the United Kingdom that the Fijians sought would be preserved in the ministerial system though precisely how was not made clear. The governor would be vested with a range of powers over advisory and statutory bodies — such as the public service and police commissions — to ensure that the interests of all the communities were protected, obviating the need for a precisely formulated pledge that the Fijians wanted. It might be counterproductive for Fijians in any case to push too hard for an 'ultimate solution' lest it unduly antagonise the Indo-Fijians and invite the attention of the United Nations.[54] The demand for Fiji to become a Christian state should be abandoned in favour of the principle of non-discrimination. London was acutely aware of the deep sensitivities on the ground in Fiji, and advised Jakeway not to commit himself to any particular cause of action before further consultation.

Jakeway was a complete contrast with Maddocks. He was energetic and involved, unlike his predecessor, who was distant and detached and often in ill health. More than personality, however, Jakeway's background was important. He had been chief secretary in British Guiana in 1956 when Cheddi Jagan's Peoples Progressive Party had accused the government of gerrymandering the division of constituencies to favour its opponent, Forbes Burnham. Surviving the controversy, Jakeway left to serve as chief secretary in the former British protectorate of Sarawak, which became part of the Malaysian Federation in 1963. In Sarawak, he came to know first hand the service of Fijian soldiers fighting the Chinese communist insurgency in the 1950s. He developed a sympathetic understanding of the problems of the Malays, and there is little doubt that he saw the Fijian dilemma through the lens of his Malayan experience, describing Fijians as a huskier version of non-Muslim Malays. In Fiji, Jakeway was active behind the scenes, advising Mara to form a multiracial political organisation along the lines of the 'Alliance' party in Malaya. In the process, Jakeway fell foul of the Indo-Fijian leaders, who petitioned London to recall him. London did not, and a politically damaged Jakeway remained to guide Fiji through its most intense and contested period of constitutional development. Whether Fiji might have taken a different turn had another person with a different background and a more impartial approach been at the helm remains an interesting question.

Fiji's first election for an expanded legislature under a new constitution, replacing that of 1937, held in April 1963. It was an important election for a number of reasons. For the first time, elections were fought on the basis of universal adult franchise, with no property qualification for voters or candidates. It was also the first time that the ballot box had reached the Fijian people, enabling them to elect their representatives directly. Until then, Fijians were sent to the Legislative Council by the Council of Chiefs. In the Fijian constituencies, all three sitting members of the council — Ratu Mara, Ratu Penaia and Semesa Sikivou — were re-elected. Among the Indo-Fijians, the contest was fiercer and more unpredictable. Emotions in the community were raw over the sugar strike of 1960, with the result that the election came to be seen effectively as a referendum on the strike and on certain people's role in it. Among them was A. D. Patel, the leader of the strike (who had been a member of the Legislative and Executive Councils from 1944 to 1950 but had retired to his flourishing private law practice after several electoral defeats in the early 1950s).[55]

Patel won the election easily along with other members of the recently formed 'Citizens Federation', James Madhavan and S. M. Koya. It was an interesting and unusual combination of a Hindu, a Christian and a Muslim representing the Indo-Fijian community, especially in view of the persistent argument that Muslims and Christians could not be elected from a predominantly Hindu electorate of the colony. Patel's re-entry galvanised the political scene. His uncompromising stand on the common roll was to become one of the most deeply contested issues during the 1960s as Fiji moved towards independence. With Patel in the council as the leader of the Indo-Fijian community, Fiji had at its helm in the mid-1960s three exceptionally talented and tough-minded men, attached — in the case of Mara and Patel — to strongly held principles, unwilling to compromise, each seeking advantage for their respective political ideologies, one demanding the recognition of 'race' as the main principle of political representation, the other striving for a non-racial political culture.

With the election over, Jakeway proceeded to prepare the colony for the introduction of the membership system. That came on 1 July 1964. The government appointed three members, a Fijian, an Indo-Fijian and a European each: J. N. Falvey became the Member for Communication and Works (part-time), Ratu Mara the Member for Natural Resources and A. D. Patel the Member for Social Services. The choice of the three was to be expected: they were the acknowledged leaders of their respective communities. Mara's portfolio included agriculture, cooperatives, fisheries, forestry, geology, lands, livestock, marketing and mining — all areas of particular concern to the indigenous community. Patel was responsible for broadcasting, cultural activities, education, health, prisons and social welfare. Falvey's portfolio, meanwhile, included meteorology, postal services, civil aviation, tourism, transport and hotels — areas in which the Europeans had major investments and interests. The members had a collective responsibility for the implementation of policy, and were answerable to the Legislative and Executive Councils for the departments under their charge. In the end, however, theirs was only an advisory role; all policy matters were the responsibility of the governor alone.

The membership system was cumbersome. It was intended to give members administrative experience within a framework of collective responsibility, but members — elected representatives of their respective ethnic communities — had their own interests to safeguard while participating in a government with whose policies they might not agree. Wires were certain to be crossed, and they were, especially between Patel, as the leader of the Indo-Fijian community, and Jakeway, as the head of government (and indeed between Patel and his own supporters).[56] As preparations began for the constitutional conference in London in 1965, the political temperature in Fiji increased. Patel's Federation Party raised issues — about common roll and independence, for instance — that aroused strong emotions. Inevitably, they came under attack from the conservative Australian-owned newspapers, in particular the *Fiji Times*, whose New Zealand-born editor, L. G. Usher, was virulently anti-Patel, according to Acting Governor P. D. Macdonald, who told the CO that Usher 'slyly hints at the unreasonableness of the attitude of the Federation group, and the rightness of the stand taken by the other groups'.[57]

The Federation Party was attacked even by the government's own public relations department, which, ironically, had been in Patel's original portfolio but was withdrawn after threats of mass European resignations. The Fiji Broadcasting Commission (FBC), a statutory body, called members of the party '*badmash*', hooligans, which they found 'abusive, insulting and provocative'.[58] The government chose to remain silent, saying that it did not know the meaning of the word and that, in any case, the FBC was a self-financing and self-regulating body.

When Patel attacked the FBC publicly, Jakeway rebuked him and demanded his resignation if he could not observe the rules of collective responsibility entailed in the membership system. How could a member of government publicly attack a branch of that government? Jakeway was determined to bring Patel into line. 'I cannot condone such flagrant violation of the principle of collective responsibility,' he informed the CO.[59] The governor wrote to Patel asking him to 'explicitly and immediately' dissociate himself from the attacks; failure to do so would 'bring into question your continued membership of Executive Council'.[60] Patel reminded the governor of the terms and conditions on which he had accepted the appointment. He could not be expected to consider himself 'responsible to defend the wrongful acts of civil servants or defend them against public criticism' when, as member for social services, he had no power himself to hold officers in his portfolio to account. He had joined the government to 'serve my people — not to forsake them; and I am not prepared to sell my soul for a mess of potage'.[61] He offered to resign if that was what the secretary of state and the governor wanted.

Patel's offer put the governor in a bind. He could, as he had indicated, accept his resignation, but that would deprive the government of the leader of the majority Indo-Fijian party in the Legislative Council, and the undisputed leader of the Indo-Fijian community in the colony. It would be a severe setback for the experiment of multiracial cooperation that the government was undertaking. Or the governor could swallow his pride and keep Patel on, though with no particular hope of eliciting active cooperation from him. Trafford Smith, assistant undersecretary of state, sympathised with Jakeway but alerted him to the 'serious and far reaching' consequences of not having Patel — and his fellow party member James Madhavan — in the Legislative Council. Might they not adopt a more extreme position, which could potentially affect race relations, internal security and effective and smooth running of government? Jakeway reluctantly heeded the advice. He wrote to Patel:

> I value your membership of Executive Council and believe it to be in the national interest that you should continue to be a member and to retain your portfolio. I realise that this from time to time presents you with a conflict of loyalties, and I have hitherto much admired the way in which you have reconciled that conflict. At this juncture, in particular, it would be a setback to the ideal of national unity for which we are both striving if the leader of the majority Indo-Fijian party withdrew from the Government.[62]

London hoped that the 'whole incident has not so seriously undermined the confidence of the other communities in the Indians as to make progress between now and the conference impossible'.[63] Its hopes were in vain.

The altercation between Patel and Jakeway could not have come at a worse time: on the eve of the constitutional conference in London. Relations between the two men, never close, became frosty. S. M. Koya, the deputy leader of the Federation Party, openly called Jakeway 'anti-Indian' and challenged his impartiality and integrity.[64] The governor's refusal to allow the Indo-Fijian community to accord a formal Indian welcome ceremony for Secretary of State, Fred Lee, dismayed many, especially when Fijians were allowed to welcome him traditionally at the chiefly island of Bau. Jakeway's statement during the course of a visit to Australia that 'it is inconceivable that Britain would ever permit the Fijian people to be placed politically under the heel of an immigrant community', and that 'the Indo-Fijians do not want self-government, because this would immediately cause racial strife', provoked a storm of protest, which did not abate quickly.[65] The Federation Party protested against the characterisation of the Indo-Fijians as an 'immigrant' community — with all the political implications it entailed at a time when the constitutional future was being decided. Jakeway's statement, the party said, had seriously prejudiced the forthcoming conference by prejudging important issues. It petitioned the CO to recall Jakeway. For his part, trying to save face, the governor responded that he had been misrepresented. He was not. London backed the governor, but worried if his 'reputation for impartiality had been substantially damaged'. For the Indo-Fijian leaders, it had.

ENDNOTES

[1] Davidson, J. W. 1966, 'Constitutional Change in Fiji', *Journal of Pacific History*, vol. 1, p. 165, had Maddocks and his senior advisors in mind, whom he accused of 'benign paternalism', of not having any 'deep sense of commitment to self-government' and of not possessing 'much political sensitivity or skill'.

[2] An admiring biography of Sukuna is by Scarr, Deryck 1980, *Ratu Sukuna: Soldier, Statesman, Man of Two Worlds*, Macmillan Education, London. Meli Bogileka, a prominent Fijian politician from western Fiji, chided Sukuna publicly for siding with the colonial administrators in keeping Fijians 'near-slavery'. See fijilive, 21 May 2005.

[3] Sir Kenneth Maddocks to P. Rogers, 24 June 1959, CO1036/307, no. 32.

[4] P. Rogers to Sir Kenneth Maddocks, 14 August 1959, CO1036.307, no. 34.

[5] Ibid.

[6] Ibid.

[7] The following quotes for Weston and Macdonald can be found in 'Brief on constitutional reform', Fijian government note sent by P. D. Macdonald to A. R. Thomas, 20 September 1960, CO1036/612, no. 6.

[8] This is discussed at length in Lal, Brij V. 1992, *Broken Waves: A History of the Fiji Islands in the 20th Century*, University of Hawai'i Press, Honolulu, pp. 108–25 (n. 3). See also Ravuvu, Asesela 1974, *Fijians at War*, Institute of Pacific Studies, Suva.

[9] 'Policy towards Fiji', 8 November 1960, CO1036, no. 11. (Reproduced as Chapter 6.)

[10] Amery's characterisation of Fiji's divided society was echoed repeatedly in official correspondence. See, for example, Sir Kenneth Maddocks' dispatch to the Colonial Office, 14 April 1961, no. 33.

[11] Minute by H. P. Hall, 8 November 1960, CO1036/865.

[12] Minute from Sir H. Poynton to Hugh Fraser, 10 November 1960, CO1036/865.

[13] See Norton, Robert 2002, 'Accommodating indigenous privilege: Britain's dilemma in decolonising Fiji', *Journal of Pacific History*, vol. xxxviii, pp. 2, 135.

[14] See Scarr (1980).

[15] Norton (2002:135 [n. 69]).

[16] 'Future of Fiji', letter from Sir H. Poynton to Sir K. Maddocks, 17 November 1960, CO1036/612, no. 17.

[17] Ibid.

[18] Ibid.

[19] Sir K. Maddocks to H. P. Hall, 17 January 1961, CO1036/612, no. 29. See also H. P. Hall to Sir K. Maddocks, 6 February 1961, CO1036/612, no. 30; and 'Fiji government proposals for constitutional reform', 27 February 1961, CO1036/612, no. 38.

[20] This and the following quotes are from the debate reported in *Fiji Legislative Council Debates* (1961).

[21] Mara's account of his career is in Mara, Ratu Kamisese 1997, *The Pacific Way: A Memoir*, University of Hawai'i Press, Honolulu.

[22] In private, however, Mara was not as dogmatic, telling the Colonial Office in October 1961 that he was 'convinced that the Fijian administration had to be overhauled and he was in favour of the establishment of multiracial local government'. He was also in favour of the introduction of the membership system, which, he said, the Fijian people themselves would come to accept in time.

[23] Minute by Sir H. Poynton to H. Fraser, 12 July 1962, CO1036/62.

[24] Ibid.

[25] Ibid.

[26] On the Fijian understanding of paramountcy, see A. C. Reid to I. S. Wheatley, 28 April 1962, CO1036/775, no. 5.

[27] P. McDonald to Mr McLeod, 21 July 1961, CO1036/613, no. 67.

[28] Minute by A. R. Thomas, 10 August 1961, CO1036/613.

[29] Dispatch from Sir K. Maddocks to Mr Maudling, 28 October 1961, CO1036/613, no. 94.

[30] Minute by A. R. Thomas, 10 August 1961, CO1036/613.

[31] Dispatch from Sir K. Maddocks to Mr Maudling, 19 June 1962, CO1036/775, no. 8.

[32] Dispatch from Duncan Sandys to Sir K. Maddocks, 31 July 1962, CO1036/775, no. 10.

[33] Minutes by J. E. Marnham, A. R. Thomas and Sir H. Poynton on future policy in the context of talks with other powers about colonial territories in the Pacific, 3–13 July 1962, CO1036/654.

[34] Dispatch (reply) from Sir K. Maddocks to Mr Sandys arguing in favour of gradual change, 10 October 1962, CO1036/775, no. 21.

[35] P. D. Macdonald to J. E. Marnham, 18 October 1962, CO1036/703, no. 16.

[36] Sir R. Garvey to J. E. Marnham, 14 November 1962, CO1036/703, no. 3.

[37] J. E. Marnham to Sir R. Garvey, 12 November 1962, CO1036/703, no. 13.

[38] Sir R. Garvey to J. E. Marnham, 14 November 1962, CO1036/703, no. 3.

[39] Minute by I. S. Wheatley, 4 December 1962, CO1036/618.

[40] Ibid.

[41] Minutes by J. E. Marnham, 6 December 1962, and A. R. Thomas, 11 December 1962, CO1036/618.

[42] Minute (reply) from C. R. Roberts to I. S. Wheatley, 6 December 1962, CO1036/618.

[43] Minute by J. E. Marnham on Fisher's brief for his visit to Fiji, 18 December 1962, CO1036/775, no. 33.

[44] Memorandum by H. G. Nicholls, Chief Inspector, CSR, Fiji, 19 January 1963, CO1036/1392, no. 5.

[45] Suva Chamber of Commerce memorandum presented to Nigel Fisher, 16 January 1963, CO1036/1392, no. 38.

[46] Fijian Cane Growers' Industrial Congress memorandum to Fisher, 12 January 1963, CO1036/1392.

[47] 'Political future of Fiji', memorandum presented to Fisher by the Fijian Western Democratic Party, January 1963, CO1036/392, no. 40.

[48] Fijian Affairs Board memorandum on Fijian rights presented to Fisher, 17 January 1963, CO1036/107, no. 8.

[49] Maddocks' dispatch to Sandys, 13 March 1963, enclosing report by Fiji Intelligence Committee, CO1036/1214, no. 5.

[50] Dispatch (reply) from Duncan Sandys to Sir K. Maddocks, 31 July 1962, CO1036/775, no. 10.

[51] 'Future Policy on Fiji', *Cabinet Paper*, 134/2403 PFP (63) 3; and *Cabinet Paper*, 134/2403 PFP 1 (63) 2.

[52] 'Strategic importance and security of the Pacific Islands Region', *Cabinet Paper*, 18 January 1963, 134/2403 PFP (63) 1.

[53] Dispatch from Duncan Sandys to Sir K. Maddocks, 15 August 1963, CO1036/1067, no. 93.

[54] J. E. Marnham to Sir D. Jakeway, 13 April 1964, CO1036/1067, no. 15.

[55] See Lal, Brij V. 1997a, *A Vision for Change: A. D. Patel and the Politics of Fiji*, National Centre for Development Studies, The Australian National University, Canberra, n. 4.

[56] I am grateful to Rod Alley for background information on Patel's difficulties with his own community over his role as member for social services.

[57] Macdonald to Greenwood, 6 August 1965, CO1036/1216, no. 83.

[58] Letter from A. D. Patel to Sir D. Jakeway, 30 April 1965, CO1036/1263, no. 24.

[59] Inward telegram from Sir D. Jakeway to Trafford Smith, 27 April 1965, CO1036/1263, no. 20.
[60] Letter from Sir D. Jakeway to Mr Patel and Mr Madhavan, 27 April 1965, CO1036/1263, no. 24.
[61] Letter from A. D. Patel to Sir D. Jakeway, 30 April 1965, CO1036/1263, no. 24.
[62] Letter from Sir D. Jakeway to A. D. Patel, 6 May 1965, CO1036/1263, no. 26.
[63] From Trafford Smith to Sir D. Jakeway, 17 May 1965, CO1036/1263, no. 26.
[64] Fiji Intelligence Report, September 1965, CO1036/1216, E/91, in which Koya is reported to have attacked Jakeway.
[65] Jakeway's statement about 'an immigrant community' is in the CO brief for Eireen White's visit to Fiji, April 1965, in Annex D, CO1036/1551.

4. The 1965 Constitutional Conference

The stand-off between Sir Derek Jakeway and A. D. Patel took place during a familiarisation visit to Fiji by parliamentary undersecretary of state, Eirene White, in what was now a Labour government in Britain. Her task was to report back on issues that might be raised at the forthcoming constitutional conference. She heard a wide range of opinion: from Muslims about separate representation, from Fijians about their special interests — including political leadership of the country — from the ever mercurial Apisai Tora about deporting Indo-Fijians as Ceylon and Burma had done, from the Council of Chiefs reiterating the terms of the Wakaya Letter, from Indian leaders about common roll and the need to promote political integration, from journalist Alipate Sikivou expressing the Fijian nationalist line that the Indians could always go back to India, the Chinese to China and the Rotumans and other islanders to their respective islands but the Fijians, the indigenous people, had Fiji as their only home. Sikivou was not alone in holding such extreme views. Many others were of the view that, as Ratu Penaia Ganilau and Ratu George Cakobau had said in 1961, at independence, Fiji should be returned to the Fijians. As Uraia Koroi put it at a meeting of the Fijian Association in January 1965, chaired by Ratu Mara, 'Fijians were determined to achieve this claim of right [returning Fiji to Fijians] at the cost of their lives. Bloodshed would mean nothing if their demands were not acceptable to other races in the Colony.'[1]

A month before White's tour, in March, Trafford Smith had visited Fiji to talk specifically to the leaders of the three communities about their attitude and possible policy stance at the London conference.[2] Ratu Mara, whom Smith found to be 'thoughtful and reserved, much less open and gay', with an 'almost donnish outlook', reiterated the complete Fijian opposition to common roll, expressed optimism on the resolution of the land-lease situation while conveying Fijian fears of being dispossessed of their ownership rights, and thought the Fijian demand for paramountcy could be accommodated perhaps by giving Fijians an extra seat. He was 'not particularly impressed by Mr Falvey's idea of a trial balloon of three Common Roll seats at the next election'. Patel, whom Smith found a 'charming man to meet, not the "bogey-man" the *Fiji Times* makes him out to be', was prone to looking 'for sinister motives in British actions which are in fact either completely innocent or unthinking', such as Jakeway's speech in Australia, which had caused a furore in Fiji. Patel told Smith of the inequities of the colonial administration, the official patronage of anti-Federation Indo-Fijians and the 'islands of autocracy' in the public sector immune from parliamentary scrutiny. For him, the main controversial issues at the conference would be the method of election and the composition of the Executive. 'Would you be prepared to move away from common roll to some kind of compromise if necessary,' Smith asked Patel at a private function. Patel answered: 'I would try to find a form of common roll having safeguards which would make it acceptable to the Fijians.' John Falvey, reputed to be 'the best brain among the Europeans', though not making much of an impression on Smith, explained the basis of Fijian–European political cooperation against the Indo-Fijians, emphasised the depth of the Fijian attachment to the principle of paramountcy, offered to give up a European seat to accommodate it and raised the possibility of three common-roll seats contested by a member of each of the three main groups.

Throughout the early 1960s, the issue of land ownership and Fijian fears of dispossession lay close to the heart of the problem in Fiji — fears accentuated by a rapid increase in the Indo-Fijian population and increasing demand for a more secure land-tenure system. If they were not in political control, Fijians feared — or at least they said they feared — Indo-Fijians would enact legislation to take their land away. Land was not only an economic and social asset, it was the source of great power and Fijians were acutely conscious of it, using it as a leverage to extract concessions in the political arena. For Indo-Fijian politicians, however, land ownership itself was not an issue; everyone respected the ownership rights of the Fijians. At issue were the terms and conditions under which Fijian land should be leased to mostly non-Fijian tenants. Fortunately, the lease issue was addressed in the report of the Agricultural Landlord and Tenant Committee, which was accepted by the CO, with slight modification.[3] New leases would be granted for a minimum of 10 years and would be inheritable. This, Trafford Smith pointed out to Jakeway, was an improvement on the English practice itself. Under the new legislation, tenants would be paid compensation for improvements they had made if the lease was not renewed, and there would be a Lands Tribunal to review rents and, perhaps more importantly, to decide on the 'relative' hardship if a lease was renewed or not renewed. As this tended to favour the tenants, the new provision came over time to be resented by many Fijians. At the time, however, the passage of the legislation caused much relief to officials in London and in Suva. In Fiji, Indo-Fijian leaders — A. D. Patel in particular — were blamed by some for 'selling out' the interests of the tenants, without appreciating the constraints of the times, the tenacity of the Fijian opposition or the subtlety of legislation that actually secured for tenants rights and privileges that no earlier legislation had done. The CO hoped privately that the resolution of the land issue might persuade the Indo-Fijian leaders to be more accommodating of the Fijian position in future negotiations.

Early in 1965, the governor initiated among members of the Legislative Council a dialogue about issues likely to be raised at the London conference. He aimed to achieve a measure of consensus, which, he hoped, would augur well for the coming talks. The discussion produced consensus on many issues: complete and immediate independence would not be the immediate aim of the conference, and links with the British Crown would be maintained. Predictably, however, the talks faltered on the perennially thorny issue of the method of election. Patel pressed his case for common roll, while the Fijians and Europeans opposed it. When distorted versions of the confidential talks began to appear in the colony's major local daily,[4] accusing Patel and his fellow members of the Legislative Council of unstatesmanlike behaviour, Patel withdrew from the talks — not only because the leaks had 'created an atmosphere of mistrust and misunderstanding among the people of Fiji', but because 'nearly all the remaining subjects for discussion are controversial and on which it is very unlikely any agreement would be reached in Fiji'.[5] The government's own intelligence unit admitted that the *Fiji Times* often published distorted and damaging versions of Patel's speeches. The breakdown had several unfortunate consequences. It deepened the rift already growing between Patel and Jakeway. It poisoned political relations between the principal protagonists and it forged ever closer relations between Fijian and European leaders, which could well have been the *Fiji Times*' intention. It probably also hardened Patel's stand against any compromise. As Jakeway informed London, the possibility of 'reaching unanimous agreement in London receded over the horizon' at the moment the Suva talks ceased.[6] Unfortunately, the governor himself had a hand in creating the impasse through his counterproductive confrontation with Patel and with his overtly pro-Fijian stance.

The London conference opened at Marlborough House on 26 July 1965. The positions of the three groups were clear.[7] The Fijian group wanted the recognition of the principle of Fijian paramountcy in the form of two additional Fijian seats — nominated by the Great Council of Chiefs — and the complete rejection of common roll, though the CO thought Fijian leaders were 'prepared to listen to proposals from the British side and to give them a fair hearing' because their 'confidence in British integrity is complete'. The Indo-Fijians wanted common roll and self-government with continuing links with the United Kingdom. The European view was identical to that of the Fijians. The UK government opted to play a disengaged role in the deliberations. The secretary of state assured the Fiji delegation 'that you will encounter no disposition on the part of the British Government to press particular solutions upon you'.[8] Ratu Mara, in his opening remarks, paid warm tribute to Britain, emphasising loyalty, trust and gratitude, saying that independence was not his goal, that he saw no reason to sever links with the Crown 'forged by our forefathers in 1874'.[9] He spoke warmly of his and his people's 'trust and abiding loyalty in the British Crown and in British institutions'. Falvey, speaking for the European but also 'with' the Fijian delegation, echoed Mara's sentiments: continuing links with the Crown, satisfaction with the status quo, gratitude for all that Britain had done for Fiji. 'There are in fact many people of all races in Fiji who are well content with our present and relatively new constitution,' he said, 'and you will find few in our country who are seriously critical of the Government and the administration of our country since 1874 when sovereignty was ceded to Her late Majesty, Queen Victoria.' These were unsurprising sentiments from one opposed to any reduction in European over-representation in the colonial legislature.

A. D. Patel predictably took a completely different line to Mara and Falvey. He hoped that the conference would produce a new constitution that would lead Fiji to 'complete independence in the not too distant future'. He spoke about the enduring importance of political freedom of the type developed democracies enjoyed. 'Political liberty, equality and fraternity rank foremost among the good things of life and mankind all over the world cherishes and holds these ideals close to its heart. The people of Fiji are no exception.' He hoped the conference would mark the 'beginning of the end of a form of government which stands universally condemned in the modern world'. He too had 'faith and trust in the British people and the UK Government' to work out a just and fair solution for Fiji, but warned that '[w]e have all got to guard ourselves against avoiding right decisions because they are unpleasant or run counter to our ingrained habits of preconditioned thought, or wrong decisions because they appear advantageous in the short run'.

Patel's anti-colonial sentiments would have been unexceptionable in most circumstances. Many in the United Kingdom felt that the days of colonial rule were numbered; and the words Patel spoke were a regular part of the vocabulary of many a nationalist leader in the Third World. But Fiji was Fiji. The British colonial system there was not reviled universally, but was embraced warmly by the indigenous population and supported opportunistically by the Europeans. It had preserved the Fijian way of life and secured their fundamental interests, such as ownership of the land. In that context, Patel's condemnation of colonialism, at the high table of the Empire, in the presence of people who were running it or wanted its essence retained or were full of praise for what it had accomplished, must have struck a jarring note. The UK delegation was already favourably disposed to the Fijian position, with the Fijian leaders making a considerable play of the Fijian contribution to World War II and the poor contribution of the Indo-Fijian community to that conflict.[10] Patel's denunciation must have disappointed and embarrassed them, to the detriment of the cause he was pursuing. Whether a more tactful approach would have yielded a different result — and encouraged the CO to seek a compromise solution acceptable to all sides — is a matter best left to speculation.[11] For their part, senior CO officials predictably sought to put the 'failure' of the conference to provide a broadly acceptable consensus outcome squarely on the shoulders of Patel and his colleagues.

The conference nevertheless produced several major steps towards greater internal self-government.[12] For the first time, the constitution provided for a majority-elected Legislative Council and the end of the nomination of unofficial members. The only nominated members in the legislature were to be the attorney-general, the financial secretary and the colonial secretary. Chinese, Rotumans and other Pacific Islanders were to be enfranchised for the first time — the Chinese placed on the European roll and the latter two on the Fijian. A new Public Service Commission and a Police Service Commission were to be created, which the governor would be required to consult, though the most senior officers — the attorney-general, financial secretary, colonial secretary and commissioner of police — would continue to be appointed by London. The constitution also for the first time would contain a bill of rights, though it did not provide protection against discrimination in civil service appointments — not surprising in view of the concern about racial imbalance there.

It was the composition of the Legislative Council and the method of election that proved, unsurprisingly, to be the most contentious issues at the conference. The council was to be expanded to 36: 14 Fijians, 12 Indo-Fijians and 10 Europeans. With the two additional members, nominated by the Council of Chiefs but who would be full members of the Legislative Council, the principle of Fijian paramountcy, which had so long divided opinion in London and in Suva, was at last recognised. The European number would be reduced by two, but given their tiny size, they would still be over-represented. London was disposed to reducing their numbers even further to appease Indo-Fijian feelings, but Fijians would not countenance further reduction: after all, Europeans were their willing and eager ally against the Indo-Fijians. The Indo-Fijians — the majority population of the colony — were to be reduced to a minority in the legislature.

The conference produced an outcome that pleased — and relieved — officials: a Fijian majority (assured because of traditional European support) and thus a Fijian chief minister. Second, the Tanganyika Model, which Maddocks had advocated so strenuously, was also introduced. Of the 12 Fijian and Indo-Fijian members, nine would be elected on separate racial rolls, now called communal rolls (seven general electors).[13] The remaining members — three general electors, Fijians and Indo-Fijians — were to be elected on a cross-voting roll where the ethnicity of the candidates would be stipulated, but they would be voted for by everyone eligible to vote, irrespective of ethnicity. There was another feature of the constitution that further isolated the Indo-Fijians from the rest of the community. For the first time, the Chinese were enfranchised, and they were placed on the general roll while Rotumans and other Pacific Islanders were placed on the Fijian roll. This amalgamation in effect turned the Fijian and European rolls into non-racial common rolls, while the Indo-Fijians remained communally separated.

The Federation Party protested against the final report of the conference. The two extra Fijian seats — through the Council of Chiefs — had upset the principle of parity between the two communities. The Tanganyika Model was unacceptable to them and inappropriate for Fiji because of its electoral provisions. 'It would not make way for, but obstruct, the introduction or the implementation of common roll in the future,' said Patel.

> It would magnify communal differences and inevitably harden the attitude of all races (including the majority race) along communal lines. Under this system, political parties will not be able to obtain the candidature of a true representative of any particular race, let alone obtain a majority of seats in the legislature to form a workable government.[14]

The fear of Indo-Fijian domination, the party argued, was more psychological than real, because the geographical distribution of the population was uneven. It continued in a similar vein, repeating all the well-known arguments. By then, however, the party was talking to itself. When the Federation Party realised that the Fijians and Europeans would not budge on common roll, that the United Kingdom would not intervene to resolve the impasse, Andrew Deoki (non-Federation member of the Indo-Fijian delegation) proposed a compromise towards the end of the conference, which he had presented earlier in Fiji. His proposal was to introduce three additional common-roll seats to the existing system of communal representation. By then, however, the Fijians had the upper hand and London had the result it desired, so the proposal was not considered because it had come 'too late'. 'Too late for what,' Patel asked, but no one was listening.

The Federation Party threatened a boycott of the final session of the conference, but did not do so 'out of respect for the Secretary of State', it said. The party accepted the outcome on protest, and put it in writing the next day to Secretary of State, Anthony Greenwood, who had been 'preoccupied with other problems during the last few days', (specifically, Aden). Patel wrote:

> It is our intention to oppose these proposals by peaceful and constitutional means. The implementation of these proposals, in our view, would create a grave racial disharmony leading to undesirable results. In this process an irreparable harm would be done to the country as a whole and we fear that goodwill, harmony and understanding which have existed among all the races in Fiji over the last 90 years would disappear forever. The responsibility for any course of events arising out of the implementation of these proposals would rest, in our view, on Her Majesty's Government.[15]

Greenwood admitted that the constitution was not perfect but thought sufficient progress had been made towards multiracialism in the cross-voting proposals and urged everyone 'to strive to make it work with the maximum efficiency for the benefit of all the people of your country', to consolidate the growth and achievement of racial harmony. An elated Ratu Mara cabled Fiji: '*Ni yalovinaka ni kakua ni taqaya, na veika kece koni taqayataka e seqa ni yaco, sa nomuni na lagilagi* [Do not be concerned. All that you were concerned about did not materialise. The victory is yours].'[16] Large victory celebrations awaited the Fijian delegation in Fiji.

Trafford Smith offered his own assessment of the conference and how it transpired as it did.[17] He reported to Jakeway that Mrs White had held private talks with Mara and Falvey during the conference to see if giving Indo-Fijians an extra seat would 'be worth the candle'. The proposal was rejected because 'a late concession of this sort might have shown that [Her Majesty's Government] — and the Fijians and Europeans, if they acquiesced — were trying to make some move towards placating the Indo-Fijians'. There was no political advantage for any of the three parties in making this concession anyway. Smith thought Patel 'got off on the wrong foot during the formal opening session by talking about independence as the ultimate objective and holding up the colonial state of Fiji to condemnation'. He also considered the Federation group singularly inept and unprepared for the conference. Had 'Patel and his henchmen'[18] tabled the compromise proposal for limited common roll at the beginning of the conference, the British government would have had to take a serious note of it and impress on the Fijians and the Europeans the need to consider it. Rarely 'has a case been so mishandled by three competent lawyers'.

Smith's tone needs to be tempered by several considerations. The UK delegation seems to have been more concerned to appease the Fijians than to arrive at a solution broadly acceptable to all parties. White held private talks with Mara and Falvey, but made no such attempts with the Indo-Fijian delegation, to impress upon them to meet the others half way. In this, she was disregarding the advice of the CO, which thought it 'necessary to have separate discussions with the delegates from each community to find out to what extent they are prepared to compromise on the issue of common roll'.[19] Accusing the Indo-Fijian delegation of not offering the compromise common-roll proposal on the first day of the conference was like asking a negotiator to put on the table their basic minimum demands at the outset of the bargaining process. For a different reason, the CO itself recommended that it was 'desirable to avoid allowing this issue [common roll] to be raised in full conference at an early stage as to do so might well lead to the striking of attitudes and deadlock'. Smith was accusing the Federation Party of taking the course of action his own office recommended! For him to argue later that the Indo-Fijian delegation should have declared hand earlier seems self-serving.

The Federation Party had hoped to convince the conference of the merits of its common-roll proposal for building a new, non-racial Fiji, and expected Britain to show some sympathy for its position. Only when that approach failed was it prudent, at the last minute, to present their minimum demand. The tactic was unexceptionable. London was, however, more attuned to the demands of the Fijians, and some members of the European delegation felt close enough socially to the officials in London to make, as Smith reported, racist, anti-Indian comments in their presence. 'We all hate Indians,' Richard Kearsely was heard to say, while Falvey called Patel a 'rat', to the discomfort and embarrassment of some CO officials.[20] Privately, senior officials in the CO, such as A. J. Fairclough, assistant secretary and head of the Pacific and Indian Ocean Department, agreed that the outcome of the 1965 constitutional conference was 'unduly pro-Fijian' — though he doubted the prospects of a truly democratic set-up in Fiji.[21] Independent experts — the eminent Commonwealth constitutional lawyer Professor Stanley de Smith among them — agreed, regretting that the Federation Party's 'relatively moderate compromise proposal [for limited introduction of common roll] received such short shrift'.[22] The 'movement must necessarily be towards a common electoral roll,' he wrote, 'with or without racial reservation of seats. The only real question is one of timing.'

Were the Fijians going to be as intransigent on common roll, as officials in London thought? A CO brief summed up Jakeway's talks with three pre-eminent Fijian leaders, Ratu Mara, Ratu Penaia Ganilau and Ratu Edward Cakobau: the governor reported that 'some gentle selling of the attractions of a limited common roll element in the next constitutional stage has been done with all three and does not appear to have fallen on entirely unreceptive ground'. It was true that the Council of Chiefs had come out in favour of a communal roll but there was no specific discussion on the electoral system. Jakeway suggested that 'the position is that they are prepared to listen to proposals from the British side and to give them a fair hearing'.[23] None came. The governor also informed London that Patel would pursue common roll, but 'if he sees no alternative, he will probably accept a limited number of common roll seats in a Legislative Council which is otherwise elected on communal roll'.

The United Kingdom went into the conference, however, with its mind already made up to recommend the adoption of three cross-voting seats on the basis of parity. The CO recommended that Fijians and Indo-Fijians have parity (12 seats each), but Fijians got two more during the conference. Once back in Fiji and stunned by the vehemence of the Indo-Fijian reaction, Jakeway broached with Mara and Falvey the possibility of Fijians reverting to the status quo, but by then it was too late, and would 'lead to too many internal difficulties for the Fijians themselves'. Nonetheless, the CO 'thumped home' to Mara and Falvey that 'it is essential for the future happiness and good government of Fiji that a vigorous attempt should be made to make a multi-racial appeal to the electorate not only in the cross-voting seats but also more generally'. Would the subsequent history of Fiji have unfolded differently had this been done in London before the final document was signed? It is difficult to tell now, but Professor J. W. Davidson's observation on the 1965 conference is worth noting. 'There is reason to believe,' he wrote from close personal observation of Fiji, 'that the Fijians could have been persuaded to abandon their demand for greater representation in the legislature than that of the Indians and to accept a simple common roll procedure for the election of the nine members to be returned by voters of all communities.'[24] Certainly, a limited introduction of common roll was a distinct possibility, but the CO was trapped by past habits of thought, publicly sympathetic to Fijian concerns and understandings of their place in the larger scheme of things in Fiji and generally unwilling to force a broadly acceptable solution for fear of jeopardising the peace. When it came to the crunch, the Indo-Fijians' demands, the CO reasoned, could be dismissed without much damage.

In September 1966, Fiji held a general election under the new constitution. It was an important contest fought for the first time between two political parties, the Federation and the Alliance. The latter was launched officially on 12 March 1966, although its component parts — the Fijian Association and the Indo-Fijian National Congress, for example — had existed before then. The Fijian Association was the foundation of the Alliance. Most Europeans and a sprinkling of Indo-Fijians also joined the party. The Alliance saw itself as a multiracial political party, unlike the Federation, which while ideologically non-racial, had its base in the Indo-Fijian community and was unable to attract many Fijian or European members. Something like the Alliance was bound to enter Fiji's political arena, but it was helped considerably by encouragement from Jakeway, who helped organise contacts.[25] As he told a sitting of the Legislative Council in 1966:

> The way is wide open for leaders of imagination, who have the interests of *all* the people of Fiji truly at heart, to build political alliances with the object of contesting elections on a common cross-racial platform and, if they win a majority of seats, forming a broad-based administration which will be effectively self-governing. I shall be only too happy to cooperate with such an administration and give it maximum freedom of action.[26]

Patel clearly was not one of Jakeway's 'leaders of imagination'.

The elections produced a massive, though expected, victory for the Alliance: 22 seats to the Federation's nine (all Indo-Fijian communal seats, none of the cross-voting ones). As the leader of the Alliance, Ratu Mara was appointed the leader of government business, while retaining his natural resources portfolio for a few months before handing it over to a general elector member of the Alliance, Doug Brown. Vijay R. Singh, Patel's most bitter opponent, with a sharp mind and an eloquent tongue, was appointed Member for Social Services, and Charles Stinson, a Suva businessman, Member for Communications and Works.

Three other elected members — Ratu Penaia Ganilau, Ratu Edward Cakobau and K. S. Reddy — were coopted to the Executive Council. This arrangement lasted until 1 September 1967, when a ministerial style of government was established with Ratu Mara as Chief Minister.

The Federation Party protested against its exclusion from the Executive Council, pointing to Paragraph 39 of the conference report, which said that the 'Governor would continue to appoint the unofficial members of the Executive Council in his discretion but would provide for appropriate representation of the various communities in the unofficial element of the Executive Council'.[27] As the Federation Party represented the Indo-Fijian community, it claimed that it was entitled to be invited into the Executive Council. Trafford Smith agreed with the Federation claim, saying the 'Secretary of State no doubt had in mind that the [Executive] Council would be formed on all-party basis as hitherto'. A resounding Alliance victory was not, however, foreseen at the time of the conference. Now with the adoption of a 'government' versus 'opposition' system, Fiji had 'crossed a major Rubicon'.[28] Ratu Mara did not want the Federation Party in government because its policies, he said, were diametrically opposed to his party's and because Federation in all probability would insist on the exclusion of Indo-Fijian members of the Alliance Party from the Executive Council as a precondition for participating. This Mara would be loathe to accept because it would in effect undermine the Indo-Fijian members of his party and hand Patel a victory of sorts.[29] In any case, Patel had in the meantime accepted the role of the leader of the opposition, and the matter was allowed to rest.

The Alliance government faced the normal teething problems of all new administrations: limited resources, unskilled personnel, demands for development from all sides, the negotiation of grants and experts from London and the politics of patronage, but for the most part it had acquitted itself well. Jakeway was concerned about the emigration of skilled people from Fiji to Canada and the United States in particular and sought CO advice on how to curtail it.[30] The government could do very little was the short reply, because any undue restriction on the movement of people would breach human rights conventions. Perhaps a bond system requiring scholarship holders and other beneficiaries of subsidised training to work in the country for a specified length of time might be the solution. The CO saw a silver lining in the departure of Indo-Fijians from Fiji: an improvement in the racial balance between the two communities.[31] When Secretary of State, Fred Lee, visited Fiji in August 1966, he alluded to other pressing problems. Among them was the need for racial integration, especially in education. In the past, this had been opposed strenuously by Fijian provincial schools, fearing that integration would submerge their unique identity into something amorphous and loathsome and threaten their cultural foundation. 'There may be room for argument about timing and methods, but not for doubt of the principle itself,' Lee concluded. He advised the people to accept change, to 'assimilate it into the structure of society without allowing tradition either to impede it or to be swept away by it'.[32]

The uncertain future facing expatriate civil service officers — employed not on permanent or pensionable terms since a new policy came into effect in 1962, but on contracts in the territories where they were serving — was also a matter of grave concern not only to the officers concerned but for the orderly transition to independence.[33] The interests and welfare of the expatriate officers had to be balanced against the imperatives of localisation. Under the existing constitution, the governor, not his elected ministers, was responsible for staff matters, but with a full ministerial form of government on the books, the equation had changed. In particular, Ratu Mara was adamantly opposed to the continuation of the old arrangement, which involved differential rates of pay for local and expatriate officers. He had himself been a victim of the old system in the early 1960s, and was determined that it should go. He wanted the Overseas Services Aid Scheme (OSAS) and Her Majesty's Overseas Colonial Service dismantled, with appropriate compensation, and all future expatriate officers employed on contract or on secondment. For obvious reasons, Mara wanted accelerated localisation.[34]

Mara's opposition caught London in a dilemma. It understood the depth of Mara's personal feeling on the issue and its political ramifications in Fiji. For that reason, it could not confront him publicly. Antagonising him at a critical moment in the transition to independence held grave dangers. Neither could London disregard the welfare of senior, long-serving civil service officers who were caught in a dilemma not of their making. Matters became more complicated with Mara's refusal to go to London to discuss the issue with ministers there. He was adamant that it be discussed in Fiji, with many like-minded colleagues, where he could resist pressure that he might have to succumb to in London. There was little London could do except 'to do everything possible to persuade Ratu Mara to see the difficulties of the course he has suggested and to accept that it is preferable that OSAS should continue, despite the problems it poses for him'.[35]

Another major area of concern for Fiji was the implication of the United Kingdom's application for entry into the European Economic Community (EEC), in particular for the future of the Commonwealth Sugar Agreement. Sugar was, and long had been, the backbone of the country's economy. There was, moreover, a political dimension to the problem as well. A major success on the sugar front would augur well for Mara politically with his fledgling support in the Indo-Fijian community. It would also undermine Patel's standing among his strongest supporters in the cane belt, which was probably why Mara withdrew an invitation to Patel to accompany him to Geneva for sugar talks. To safeguard

Fiji from any potential fallout from Britain's entry into the EEC, Mara revived his 'integration' proposals. Britain was not encouraging and Mara dropped the idea, but privately, London conceded that some form of associate-state status was 'probably the right goal for Fiji'.[36] Associated status was in any case preferable to independence, a point that was not to be divulged to Mara when he came to the UK in September 1967 as part of a world tour.

The recommendation to avoid independence if possible was made after a further round of official talks about the Pacific in Washington in April 1967 involving the United Kingdom, the United States, Australia and New Zealand. The UK delegation was led by Trafford Smith. The talks proved to be detailed and, in the case of the United States, unusually candid. While admitting that Washington had yet to formulate clear policies for the Pacific, US officials made clear that they preferred association arrangements to independence. This was a view shared by the Australian delegation and Australia emerged at the talks as the most beleaguered of the four powers. Nauru and Papua New Guinea were onerous responsibilities, and the stand taken on both by the UN Committee of Twenty-Four was resented in Canberra. All four powers — New Zealand to a lesser extent — were concerned to limit UN involvement in the region. A major preoccupation of the Australians was the danger of penetration by 'hostile influences'; 'Indonesia and Asian communists seemed uppermost in their minds,' according to the UK report on the talks. The Australians also claimed to have a 'national interest' in Fiji's stability. They regarded Fiji as 'the key to the island region', and they voiced strong opposition to 'any forward movement there'. Throughout the talks, the UK delegation steered a middle course, emphasising that stability in the Pacific was a concern of all four powers; individually their aim should be to avoid 'competitive constitutional escalation' and to consider the interests of other powers in making decisions about their own territories.[37]

Two observations might be made about the wider significance of the Washington talks in April 1967. First, despite the claim to have a national interest at stake, Australia appeared less keen to involve itself in assisting financially with Fiji's development plans. The suspicion always lurked in Canberra that the United Kingdom was seeking to offload its Pacific responsibilities.[38] Secondly and rather unexpectedly, Nauru, the subject of extended discussion in Washington, became an independent republic in January 1968. With an area of only eight square miles and a population of just 5561 (an 'English village', according to officials in London), Nauru was perhaps the best example of where — according to the criteria established in Washington — independence was to be avoided. The United Kingdom went along with the decision to grant independence, believing that if Australia and the United States — who had more at stake in the Pacific — were prepared to acquiesce, it made little sense for the United Kingdom to object. By implication, if Nauru could become independent, so could Fiji.

Earlier, in February 1967, Herbert Bowden, secretary of state for Commonwealth affairs, visited Fiji as part of a familiarisation tour of the South Pacific. He gave assurances that the new departmental arrangements in Whitehall — Jakeway described the merger of the CO and Commonwealth Relations Office as a 'betrayal' of dependent territories[39] — did not mean any change in the British government's policy on Fiji.[40] Britain would not rush Fiji to independence, but would act only if Fiji asked for and was ready for it. It was advisable, he said, for Fiji to progress gradually.[41] On the future of the contested constitution, Bowden said that since it had been in existence for a short while, 'it should be given a chance to work and see if it is a viable one that meets the needs of Fiji'. On the surface it appeared an innocuous statement, but the words angered the Federation Party, which had accepted the constitution under protest in the first instance, had been politically disadvantaged by it and was committed publicly to its revocation. Patel recalled a conversation — which the CO denied ever took place — in which Anthony Greenwood allegedly said that the 1965 constitution would have a short life of two years after which another constitution would be drawn up.[42] The prospect of the contested constitution having a longer life caused him alarm. As Patel put it, if the constitution was not changed immediately, the Indo-Fijian community would be consigned to 'the wilderness of frustrated and possibly endless opposition'.[43]

Patel's criticism of the apparently unilateral manner in which the Alliance government conducted itself, hastily using the guillotine in the legislature to cut off debate on important issues — a charge steadfastly denied by Mara and the governor — soured political relations even further. So, on 1 September 1967, exactly a year after the elections, Patel moved a motion in the Legislative Council rejecting the constitution and asking for a fresh conference to devise a new constitution. The longest single-sentence motion in the history of the Fijian Legislative Council read:

> Undemocratic, iniquitous and unjust provisions characterise the existing constitution and electoral laws of Fiji and their operation have caused alarm in the minds of right thinking people and have hampered the political advancement of Fiji along democratic lines and this House therefore is of the opinion that Her Majesty's government of the United Kingdom should call a constitutional conference immediately to ensure that a new constitution is worked out and based on true democratic principles without any bias or distinction on the grounds of colour, race, religion or place of origin or vested interest, either political, economic, social or other so that Fiji may attain self-government and become a nation with honour, dignity and responsibility as soon as possible.[44]

As Vijay R. Singh was replying to the motion on behalf of the Alliance, condemning it in ringing terms, the Federation Party walked out.

The boycott caught everyone by surprise and complicated London's plans for a gradual transfer of power at a pace acceptable to the Fijians. The boycott gave rise to the need for by-elections for the Indo-Fijian members. The Federation Party's by-election platform was a reiteration of its demand during the 1966 election for complete and immediate independence for Fiji on the basis of common roll. 'Independence Our Salvation', the party's election slogan had said. The Federation Party was out to prove that the overwhelming majority of Indo-Fijians rejected the constitution. The occasion also provided the Alliance Party, and Ratu Mara in particular, the opportunity to test their strength in the Indo-Fijian community and to prove that they too had a substantial base of support. Mara told the CO that he was optimistic of making inroads into the Indo-Fijian electorate,[45] expecting to win one or two Indo-Fijian communal seats. The Indo-Fijians were beginning to realise that 'he was genuinely determined to safeguard their interests', he said. He was receiving support from Indo-Fijian workers and Gujarati businessmen opposed to Patel, but not from the Indo-Fijian middle classes, who saw better prospects for advancement under the Federation Party. Patel was himself 'clearly losing ground', Mara said hopefully.

Mara's optimistic assessment of his political support among Indo-Fijians was misplaced for — and not for the first time — the by-elections returned all the nine Federation members with increased majorities (from 65 per cent of the Indo-Fijian communal votes in 1966 to 76 per cent in 1968), with Patel returning with the largest majority of them all.[46] The Federation's win came as a result of the party representing itself as the only authentic voice of the Indo-Fijian community, its superior list of candidates compared with those of the Alliance, a professional campaign and a promise to secure a new sugarcane contract favouring the grower. The tension and animosity and the solid Indo-Fijian support for the Federation Party and the dismal performance of the Alliance among Indo-Fijians — Mara's strenuous efforts to woo them over notwithstanding — took Fiji to the brink of racial riots amid loud calls to deport Indo-Fijian leaders, and to cancel land leases to Indo-Fijian tenants. The fragile experiment in multiracialism was tested. Patel had proved his point that he was the dominant leader of the Indo-Fijian community, who could not be ignored or sidelined in any future constitutional negotiation. This proof had come, however, at a great cost to race relations, and hardening attitudes on the Fijian side that saw the increased support for the Federation Party as an Indo-Fijian attempt to control political power. The Fijian determination to stand their ground and not concede to demands that might threaten their interests was also out in the open. The Fijian leaders also realised the realities on the ground. They could not oppose independence for ever. It would be better for them to negotiate independence while they controlled the government. They therefore shifted to a stance aiming for early independence, with them in control. The by-election was the sobering wake-up call to all parties to begin negotiations on a more realistic basis.

Throughout the 1960s, London hoped that it might be able to resolve Fiji's constitutional and political problems outside the glare of international scrutiny, and it devoted a great deal of its diplomatic energy to that end — at the United Nations as well as with fellow members of the Commonwealth (not to mention the UK Parliament itself). It was not entirely successfully, for Fiji frequently came to the attention of the UN Committee of Twenty-Four throughout the decade. The committee had shown intermittent interest in Fiji earlier, but after the 1965 conference, it did so with the active encouragement and even lobbying of the Federation Party, which alleged misconduct of government and breaches of undertaking by the United Kingdom.[47] In 1968, Fiji was on the committee's agenda, in the unexpected and uncongenial company of the Portuguese colonies, French Somaliland, British Honduras and the Falkland Islands.[48] There were many issues that had the potential to cause severe embarrassment to the governments in London and Suva, including the racial system of voting, European over-representation in the legislature and the delaying of independence.

Fijian leaders had always dismissed the committee as a nuisance that should not be allowed to visit Fiji at all, but Britain could not afford to take that position. 'We should aim to be as forthcoming as we can,' the CO advised when inquiries came from the committee, 'some of the questions posed do raise difficulties, particularly as regards any premature disclosure of the substance and timing of changes to the constitution.'[49] As broad policy, the Commonwealth Office suggested that on matters of further constitutional development, London should say that it would listen to the Alliance government's proposals for the extension of cross-voting, which were under consideration, and that the gross over-representation of Europeans in the legislature would be corrected at the next constitutional conference. The aim was to deflect attention from Fiji with soothing words of reassurance about timely constitutional advancement. The UK delegation at the United Nations found a surprisingly friendly ally in India, which had accepted the UK 'argument that pressure to introduce a common franchise would jeopardise the fragile dialogue in Fiji',[50] and which encouraged moderation on debates and resolutions concerning Fiji. Mara's own chance meeting with Indira Gandhi, India's prime minister, in Malaysia and favourable reports of Mara's multiracial posture by the Indian High Commissioner in Fiji, all contributed to India diluting its former hardline position on Fiji.[51] For the time being at least, it suited the United Kingdom to have support from New Delhi.

ENDNOTES

[1] Fiji Special Branch report of a Fijian Association meeting, 18 January 1965, CO1036/1215, no. 71.

[2] 'Interviews with political leaders in Fiji', a note by Trafford Smith, March 1965, CO1036/1551, no. 1.

[3] Letter from Trafford Smith to Sir D. Jakeway, 31 August 1964, CO1036/1458, no. 64.

[4] L. G. Usher, editor of the *Fiji Times*, was suspected widely of having done the leaking. See Governor to Secretary of State, 6 August 1965, CO1036/1216, E/1/85 at 83.

[5] Lal, Brij V. 1992, *Broken Waves: A History of the Fiji Islands in the 20th Century*, University of Hawai'i Press, Honolulu, p. 197 (n. 3).

[6] Sir D. Jakeway to Trafford Smith, 16 November 1965, CO1036/1054, no. 12, enclosing draft address to the Legislative Council.

[7] CO note on the views of the Fijian delegates, July 1965, CO1036/1127, no. 3.

[8] Opening address by Mr Greenwood, 26 July 1965, CO1036/1128, no. 1.

[9] The three opening speeches by Ratu Mara, John Falvey and A. D. Patel are in CO1036/1128, no. 1, 26 July 1965.

[10] I owe this connection to Rod Alley.

[11] See, however, Norton, Robert 2002, 'Accommodating indigenous privilege: Britain's dilemma in decolonising Fiji', *Journal of Pacific History*, vol. xxxviii, p. 155 (n. 69), where he writes that Patel's rigidity was a 'strategic error'.

[12] Constitutional conference report (FCC 965) 15 (Final), 9 August 1965, CO1036/1129, no. 18.

[13] The term 'general elector' referred to anyone who was not designated Indo-Fijian, European or Pacific Islander. It included, among others, Europeans, part-Europeans and Chinese, though the Europeans exercised the dominant influence.

[14] See Lal, Brij V. 1997a, *A Vision for Change: A. D. Patel and the Politics of Fiji*, National Centre for Development Studies, The Australian National University, Canberra, p. 192 (n. 4).

[15] Note by the Indian group, July 1965, CO1036/1129, ff. 55–61. Patel's letter to Anthony Greenwood is in Lal (1997a:209–11 [n. 4]).

[16] Quoted in Lal (1992:199 [n. 3]).

[17] Letter from Trafford Smith to P. D. Macdonald, 17 August 1965, CO1036/1119, no. 73.

[18] It is important to point out that Deoki, who made the proposal, was strongly anti-Patel.

[19] CO note on the views of the Fijian delegation, July 1965, CO1036/1127, no. 3.

[20] Letter from Trafford Smith to P. D. Macdonald, 17 August 1965, CO1036/1119, no. 73.

[21] Minute by A. J. Fairclough, 9 January 1967, CO1036/1667, no. 6.

[22] Report on a visit to Fiji, August 1968, FCO32/429.

[23] Letter (reply) from Trafford Smith to Sir D. Jakeway, 13 December 1965, CO1036/1067, no. 47.

[24] Davidson, J. W. 1966, 'Constitutional Change in Fiji', *Journal of Pacific History*, vol. 1, p. 167 (n. 57).

[25] Letter from Trafford Smith to Sir D. Jakeway, 14 December 1965, CO1036/1067, no. 47.

[26] Sir D. Jakeway to Trafford Smith, enclosing draft address to Legislative Council, 16 November 1965, CO1036/1054, no. 12.

[27] Conference report (FCC65) 15 (Final), 9 August 1965, CO1036/1129, no. 18.

[28] 'Membership of the Executive Council', by Trafford Smith to Sir A. Galsworthy, 18 January 1967, FCO32/18.

[29] 'Fiji: Alliance Party government', dispatch from Sir D. Jakeway to Mr Thomson, 11 January 1968, FCO32/37.

[30] 'Emigration from Fiji', letter from C. A. Axworthy to A. J. Coles, 8 March 1966, CO1036/1645, no. 4; also, Reply, 27 April 1966, CO1036/1645, no. 5.

[31] Letter from H. P. Hall to Sir D. Jakeway, 15 November 1965, CO1036/1510, no. 2.

[32] Suva broadcast by Lee during his Pacific tour, 22 August 1966, CO1036/1721, no. 33.

[33] A brief on staffing problems prepared by the Ministry of Overseas Development, 18 July 1966, CO1036/1663, no. 13.

[34] 'Fiji: Overseas Aid Scheme', 26 February 1968, FCO32/23, no. 108.

35 Ibid.

36 'Fiji integration proposals', minute by A. J. Fairclough to Mr Bowden, 20 June 1967, FCO32/59.

37 'Pacific Island talks: Commonwealth Office notes on four-power talks in Washington', April 1967, FCO32/343.

38 'Fiji and Australia: Commonwealth Office note on Australian aid to Fiji', 30 July 1968, FCO32/364, no. 8; also FCO32/364, no. 9.

39 'Merger of Commonwealth Office and Foreign Office', letter from Sir D. Jakeway, 29 April 1968, FCO77/32.

40 Broadcast by Bowden in Fiji, 13 February 1967, FCO32/36, no. 79.

41 Commonwealth Office talking points for Bowden's visit to Fiji, February 1967, FCO32/11, no. 2.

42 Patel's letter to Greenwood is in Lal (1997a:209–11 [n. 4]).

43 Lal (1992:201 [n. 3]).

44 See Lal (1997a:229 [n. 4]).

45 A. J. Fairclough to Sir D. Jakeway, 29 June 1967, FCO32/59, no. 6, enclosing record by O. G. Foster of a meeting between Bowden and Mara.

46 For a discussion of the by-elections, see Anthony, J. M. 1969, 'The 1968 by-elections', *Journal of Pacific History*, vol. 4, pp. 132–5.

47 Letter from J. H. Lambert (head of UN Political Department in FO) to J. D. B Shaw (UK Mission to the United Nations, New York), 10 September 1968, FCO32/31, no. 35.

48 J. D. B Shaw to A. M. Warburton (FO), 24 June 1968, FCO32/31, no. 8.

49 'Fiji and the Committee of 24', minute by Sir A. Galsworthy, 10 July 1968, FCO32/31, no. 14.

50 Norton, Robert 2004, 'Seldom a transition with such aplomb: From confrontation to conciliation on Fiji's path to independence', *Journal of Pacific History*, vol. 39, no. 2, p. 171.

51 For more on this, see ibid., pp. 170–1 (n. 171).

5. Towards Independence

The 1968 by-elections changed the political dynamics in Fiji, with London acknowledging that 'the circumstances in Fiji are against us'.[1] For their part, the Fijian leaders realised that they could not expect to drag their feet over constitutional reform and continue to expect sympathetic understanding and support either from London or from younger Fijians who favoured a quicker move to full internal self-government, even independence. In the past, London had feared Fijian insurrection if changes it introduced did not meet their approval; now it was anxious that Patel's successors — 'people of a different calibre' — might resort to strongarm tactics, or even 'have recourse to violence'.[2] The Special Branch had reported that Apisai Tora, the militant western Fijian leader, had been offered a large sum of money allegedly by Siddiq Koya 'if he would pledge his support for certain courses of action', including 'physical persuasion'.[3] After the 1965 conference, Koya had threatened to break away from the Federation Party against Patel's 'passive attitude' and non-violent approach to the outcome of the conference, and was talking about forming a 'Subhas Party' — after the Indian nationalist leader Subhas Chandra Bose, who was committed to overthrowing the British in India by force — and engaging in massive civil disobedience, such as burning cane.[4] Relations between Patel and Koya, the leader and his lieutenant, were tested.[5]

In December 1968, Jakeway left Fiji, telling London on the eve of his departure to eliminate the communal rolls and replace them with cross-voting. He was supported by his chief secretary, Lloyd, who had reached similar conclusions against a constitution that, in his view, had 'an admittedly undemocratic and unsatisfactory electoral system'.[6] Jakeway was succeeded by Sir Robert Foster. Before becoming the Governor of Fiji, Foster had been the High Commissioner of the Western Pacific (1964–68). He had come to the Pacific after long service in Africa as district officer and provincial commissioner in Northern Rhodesia and as secretary of native affairs and eventually deputy governor of Nyasaland (1963–64). Fiji began its journey towards independence with Maddocks' African experiences and it was concluding it with Foster's similar background.

Six months before Foster took office, London had been considering the effects of the by-elections and exploring ways of reforming — or rejecting — a constitution it knew was flawed in favour of something more democratic and more broadly acceptable. It was with this goal in mind — to encourage fresh thinking and to contemplate alternatives — that Professor Stanley de Smith, who had advised the CO on constitutional matters in Africa, was sent to Fiji in July 1968. Professor de Smith spent a week in Fiji talking to government officials and political leaders. His extensive report was tough and insightful.[7] The 1966 constitution had two major defects, he said: it entrenched communalism and over-represented Europeans (1.4 per cent of the population holding 25 per cent of all elected seats). Separate racial representation could work perhaps as a transitional measure, but 'most of the countries in which it has been adopted at one time or another (e.g. India, Ceylon, Cyprus, Kenya) have had a depressing record of intercommunal violence'. Any constitution, to be workable, had to be practicable as well as realistic and attuned to local interests and hopes and aspirations as well as to the principles of equity and justice.

With that in mind, de Smith mooted what he called a 'Radical Approach' and a 'Realistic Approach'. The former proposed an enlarged legislature with two Fijians elected by the Council of Chiefs, but the rest elected in a mixture of some single-member and mostly two-member constituencies on a common roll, without racial reservation of seats. Communalism would be gone as an organising political principle, and parties would be forced to nominate people of different ethnicities. de Smith realised, however, that this proposal would be unacceptable, because it introduced an element of unpredictability in the outcome of elections and removed guaranteed representation on a racial basis. His realistic approach, following the Kenyan example, also comprised an enlarged legislature of 45 seats elected on a common roll and six reserved seats, two for the representatives of the Council of Chiefs and four reserved for 'general' candidates.

This approach, which 'aroused a great deal of interest', was open to criticism. The Federation Party would object, and so might the Fijians, while the question of which minority groups should receive 'special protection' could potentially open a divisive debate. The third — and for de Smith the least attractive approach — involved an extension of cross-voting seats with racial reservation. One point stands out in de Smith's proposals, no doubt reflecting his intimate knowledge of the African experience: the need to move away from communalism to a non-racial electoral system. In this respect, he was closer to Patel than to Ratu Mara and the Europeans. For his part, Jakeway favoured eliminating communal voting altogether and extending cross-voting or any other system which, as his chief secretary, Peter Lloyd, put it, could be 'cloaked with respectability' and was 'defensible internationally'.[8]

Soon after the by-elections, an Indian government minister (Sukhlal Hathi) and three senior officials from the Indian Ministry for External Affairs (Rikhi Jaipal, T. N. Kaul and Manjit Singh) visited Fiji. Hathi and Singh 'offered disinterested assistance' in healing the political and racial divide accentuated by the walkout and the by-elections. During the course of their visit, they met a wide cross-section of leaders, including Ratu Mara, who told London that he 'had recently had considerable cooperation from New Delhi'.[9] Soon after his Fiji visit, Hathi, who was India's Minister for Labour, Employment and Rehabilitation, wrote to Mara: 'I have returned to India with a feeling of optimism in regard to the future of Fiji. I have no doubt that with your wise and tolerant approach, the current difficulties in Fiji are bound to be resolved satisfactorily.'[10] Kaul and Jaipal advised the Federation Party to cooperate and abandon their boycott of the Legislative Council. Kaul also offered advice on a possible compromise formula for a new electoral system: 15 Fijian and Indo-Fijian seats each, five general seats and five 'other' seats.[11] Precisely what 'other' meant — whether they might be filled through election or by the governor through nomination, whether the elections for them would take place from single or multiple-member constituencies — became a matter of considerable debate.

Kaul refused himself to provide further clarification, saying that he had confined himself to principles, including the extension of cross-voting, a reduction in the number of European seats and parity of representation between Fijians and Indo-Fijians. Patel interpreted the Kaul formula to mean that 35 of the seats would be cross-voted, and the remaining five would be elected on a common-roll basis from single-member constituencies, with no racial reservation. The five common-roll seats would provide the opportunity for political parties to compete for votes on non-racial grounds. Patel was in the process of discussing his understanding of the Kaul formula with Ratu Mara when he (Patel) died. India's contribution in counselling moderation at the United Nations was appreciated, along with its emissaries' role in thawing relations between Mara and Patel. As the difficulties dissipated, London discouraged further direct contact for fear of losing control of the evolving negotiations, even to the point of advising Fijian officials against effusing to accept invitations to be guests of the Government of India.

That the Indo-Fijians wanted an early constitutional conference was not surprising. What did surprise Suva and London was that Fijians themselves were now demanding the same thing, though for very different reasons.[12] Their demand was based on a pragmatic assessment of the political realities on the ground. First, Fiji could not forever remain immune from international scrutiny or protected from proportional representation or majority rule, both of which were unacceptable to the Fijians. Full internal self-government would remove Fiji from UN scrutiny, the pressure of which could not be resisted for too long. Therefore 'internal self-government should be sought at the earliest possible date'. Second, the Indo-Fijian population was increasing, and further delay would make it more difficult for Fijians to insist that the political control of Fiji be handed over to them or at least to a 'political structure in which Fijian influence is paramount'. Third, once 'the complete control of internal affairs has been handed back to a body which is acceptable to Fijian opinion, Fijian interests can be protected without external interference'. The impatience of some younger prominent Fijians, such as Ratu David Toganivalu and Rusiate Nayacakalou, with the procrastination of their political leaders and Mara's aloof and dictatorial stance, also played a part. If the Alliance did not take Fiji to independence,

Nayacakalou told Toganivalu, the Federation Party would. The public stand of Fijian leaders was: no independence, at least not yet, no common roll and deep gratitude to the United Kingdom; but privately attitudes were changing or at least were more flexible. Mara's erratic and sometimes contradictory attitude to independence was calculated. He wanted to extract maximum concessions from London for his people, and for his vision of a race-based electoral system for Fiji.

By mid-1969, it was becoming clear in London and in Suva that a conference to decide a new constitution for a fully self-governing — if not completely independent — Fiji would have to be held sooner rather than later, especially in view of agreement on this by both the major parties. Officials began also to turn their minds to solutions for the issues that still divided the two parties. Full common roll and single-member constituencies were considered unrealistic because they were unacceptable to the Fijians. As G. T. P. Marshall, second secretary at what was now the Foreign and Commonwealth Office (FFCO) wrote, the

> Fijians cannot afford to take the risk that voting may develop along non-racial lines since there is too much at stake for them to be wrong. These arguments of the Fijians can never be adequately countered because there always comes a point when logic is swept aside and emotion is given free reign.[13]

With the 1969 riots in Malaysia fresh in his mind, Ratu Mara seemed wedded to the 'Bahamas' model, which provided for a large measure of internal self-government, with certain powers — external affairs, internal security, the police force and the public service — retained by the Crown, but with the provision for devolution of these responsibilities to the elected government.[14] The idea of an upper house to address Fijian concerns was also mooted, but the government was uncertain whether this would be acceptable to the Federation Party and whether it would really solve the problem of the two additional Fijian members in the Legislative Council. London knew, moreover, that upper houses were 'rather out of fashion' and generally ineffective. Surveying the overall position, the FCO commented, '[W]e are necessarily still working to a large extent in the dark.'[15] In the end, the Federation Party became a staunch advocate of the idea of an upper house with Fijian veto power, as the negotiations between the two parties gathered momentum.

Ratu Mara visited London in May 1969 and held a series of meetings with officials from the CO.[16] His discussions covered the politics and problems of defining electoral boundaries, the structure of the public service commission and similar matters. The CO also warned Mara that his proposal to perpetuate communal voting would cause problems not only in the United Nations but with members of the British Parliament, who were 'sincere advocates of the one man, one vote democratic concept [and who] would regard a pattern of communal voting as a retrograde step'. They pleaded with him to consider reducing the number of communal seats and increasing the cross-voting ones. Mara gave no undertaking but promised to discuss the proposal with Patel. Mara's London talks also touched on the implications for Fiji of the UK's entry into the EEC.[17] Dissatisfied with the assurances he was given, Mara mused sullenly about the worth of Fiji's loyalty to the United Kingdom and wondered whether Fiji would be better off to move to full independence rather than remain in a relationship doomed to fail under the pressure of economic self-interest on Britain's part. London promised to give its position in writing.[18] It also agreed to send a minister to Fiji to assess for himself the degree of agreement the two parties had reached on outstanding issues — the electoral system among them — before a new constitutional conference could be held. London had learned its lesson in 1965; it could not risk the prospect of another failed, divisive constitutional conference.

In August 1969, representatives of the Alliance and Federation parties began a series of informal, secret talks about a new constitution for Fiji to identify areas of agreement and disagreement between them.[19] In an atmosphere marked by cordiality, the leaders talked frankly and freely about their concerns and fears. A. D. Patel, who died a month after attending the first meeting, pressed his case for common roll and immediate full independence. After his death, Patel was succeeded by Siddiq Koya, also a lawyer by training, who proved less doctrinally or ideologically committed to common roll, and who was more conciliatory. Mara's relations with Koya were more cordial than they had ever been with Patel, whose guile he feared but for whose intellect and integrity he had the highest respect.[20] Having grown up at the dawn of Gandhi's anti-colonial movement, and deeply influenced by its philosophy, Patel was committed to the idea of a non-racial society to the point of stubbornness.[21] Koya, on the other hand, accepted the reality on the ground and sought to work within its parameters and constraints, whereas his predecessor had sought to change them. In the long term, however, as Fijian history shows, it was Patel's vision for Fiji that was vindicated, not the compromised Mara–Koya one.

Between August 1969 and March 1970, the secret meetings identified many areas of agreement: on the protection of Fijian interests in an upper house, on moving straight to dominion status without going through an interim period of full internal self-government and on citizenship.[22] The idea of an upper house and a move straight to independence had originated with the Federation Party.[23] The outstanding issue remained the method of election. By October, Mara was telling the governor — to the latter's considerable astonishment — that the existing (1966) constitution 'was now outlived and we should proceed as soon as possible to full independence'. While talking amicably to Indo-Fijian leaders, however, Mara was not averse to playing the nationalist card with an eye, no doubt, to extracting as many concessions from the British as possible. It was the United Kingdom that had brought Indians to Fiji, he said on one occasion, and their fate was London's responsibility, not that of the Fijian people. The United Kingdom 'had better see that arrangements reached left Fijians in control or there would be real trouble in the country'.[24]

Sir Leslie Monson, deputy undersecretary of state at the FCO whose departmental responsibilities included the Pacific and Indian Ocean, visited Fiji on a familiarisation tour in October. Before leaving, he told Lord Shepherd that for moral and 'realistic' reasons, the United Kingdom should strive for a constitutional arrangement that left the Fijians in control. His justifications were almost identical to those of Julian Amery in 1960. The realistic argument was that the dominance of Fijians in the police and armed forces and their ability — if they were so minded — to create an 'intolerable security situation', could not be discounted in any political discussion. The moral argument was the connection with the Deed of Cession. Disadvantaging the Indo-Fijians in such an arrangement was potentially risky, but it was the lesser risk of the two possible courses.[25] A draft about Fiji policy was also prepared for the Cabinet's Defence and Overseas Policy Committee.[26] Here the options open to the United Kindgdom were examined in detail. Independence on the basis of Fijian paramountcy was recommended. '[W]e will not in the end be able to justify, either in conscience, or in political terms, in our own country, a solution that does not ensure that independence will leave Fijians in control.' If Fijians did not get paramountcy, 'the risk is that they will take by force and by unconstitutional means that which they consider to be theirs. This could produce an extremely serious internal security situation, in which we should have difficulty in protecting the Indian community.' Indo-Fijians would have to be content with strong constitutional protection of their basic human rights. In time,

> the Indian side will concede that Fiji should go to independence under a constitution which would, at any rate for a time, give the Fijian side a constitutional advantage. This is the best for which we could hope ... and do not think we should give up any opportunity of achieving this because of our anxiety to relieve ourselves early of our defence and internal security responsibilities for the area.

The draft did not go to the committee, it being decided that Monson should visit Fiji first and then report back. The recommendation in favour of independence on the basis of Fijian paramountcy had one significant consequence. Officials believed that the Indian government would in all probability resent this decision. It would see it as consigning Fiji's Indo-Fijians to the status of second-class citizens. It might also think that it had been misled, deliberately, by the United Kingdom. The FCO was confident that the United Kingdom could manage any Indo-Fijian protests but also decided that now was the time to disengage from any further consultation with India about Fiji's affairs. From New Delhi, the British high commissioner concurred. The Indian connection, which had provided the United Kingdom with valuable diplomatic support at the United Nations and elsewhere and had played a role in facilitating direct talks between the Fijian and Indo-Fijian leaders, had now outlived its usefulness.[27]

In Fiji, Monson held a series of meetings with representatives of the Alliance and Federation parties and heard a range of essentially entrenched views, with some exceptions.[28] Perhaps the great change was the increased willingness of the Federation Party to compromise. The personal chemistry between Ratu Mara and Koya was an important factor in the new equation.[29] Mara found Koya easier to work with and, unlike Patel, Koya expressed high regard for Mara and showed a sympathetic understanding of his predicament. Afraid that London might force some variation of common roll on Fiji, Mara, perhaps not entirely seriously, hinted at a unilateral declaration of independence to pre-empt the issue. The Federation Party had not abandoned its common-roll platform, but the urgency was gone. In a secret discussion paper, the party proposed adopting Fijian customs and traditions as national traditions as a mark of respect for things indigenous, an upper house (made up of 13 hereditary seats occupied by the direct descendants of those who had ceded Fiji to the United Kingdom and 15 others of whom five had to be indigenous Fijians) and an elected indigenous Fijian head of state.

Monson's report on his trip covered several themes. The Fijian economy was self-sustaining, with consequential reduction in the political temperature; there was greater rapport between the two main political parties and their leaders; and it was appropriate for the United Kingdom to step aside while political leaders sought mutually acceptable solutions to their problems. Mara's personality was beginning to cause concern, Monson reported. He commented on Mara's 'habit of evading discussions which run contrary to his pre-conceived and ill-tutored ideas', his sense of personal insecurity and a growing impatience with his authoritarian style of leadership among other Fijian leaders, who might in time contemplate 'ditching' him 'for a less complex and more self-confident Fijian'.[30] He seemed also to be turning against the United Kingdom because the FCO would not contemplate a defence agreement with Fiji to maintain internal security.[31]

To FCO officials, Mara's behaviour was becoming erratic, in contrast with his earlier amiability. They commented on his moodiness, his deeply held grievances against real and imaginary wrongs and his temper tantrums. His more recent confidence and assertion of independence were, however, the result of his steadily growing stature, and a sense of personal indispensability to continuing dialogue about Fiji's future. His warming relations with Indo-Fijian leaders lessened — though did not completely remove — the need for outside mediation.

With the Federation Party concessions coming unexpectedly and all his main fears allayed, particularly in regard to common roll, Mara needed the United Kingdom less now than in the past. His growing confidence in his own authority — he was opposed to his fellow Alliance ministers meeting Monson — and his warm relations with the opposition was reflected in his call for the penultimate constitutional conference to be held in Fiji itself, not London.

In the early months of 1970, the inter-party talks produced a large measure of consensus among the leaders. On the most contentious issue that had long divided the two parties — the electoral system — Federation agreed that it would present its case in London, but would not wreck the conference over, it by suggesting that between independence and the next elections an independent commission might be appointed to examine the subject and make recommendations for the future. This was postponing the problem, Koya admitted, but he would be the 'last one to destroy his bi-partisan attitude towards the inception of common roll'.[32] Other Federation concessions were in the offing, initiated by them, Mara told Sir Robert Foster, rather than demanded by the Alliance.[33] Fiji should proceed to full dominion status soon after the constitutional conference in London, with the office of chief minister and council of ministers replaced by the office of prime minister and cabinet. The questions of electoral boundaries and method of election would be settled after independence.

Fiji would go to independence without holding an election. 'It is fully appreciated by the Opposition that this proposal gives a position of advantage to the Government of the day,' Mara informed Foster. 'They [Federation] accept this and have said they will fully support a Prime Minister during the period when final details are being worked out, particularly with regard to elections.'[34] This was precisely the outcome that the Fijian leaders had long wanted and the United Kingdom had fervently hoped for: Fijian leaders, in control, taking Fiji to independence. When a clearly surprised governor probed him about the concessions he had made, Koya explained that he had proposed the idea of an election after independence because he did not want the prevailing cordial atmosphere disrupted, that he wanted a completely successful conference (unlike 1965), that he 'thoroughly trusted' Mara and that he preferred to go to independence with him rather than someone else an election might throw up. As for common roll, Koya said he understood the Alliance leader's position and would be happy if 'Mara would say that although it is not possible to have it now, it is not ruled out for all time and in 5, 10, or 15 years it will probably be possible'. Many in the Federation Party hierarchy — though not its general secretary, Karam Ramrakha — shared that view.

London was satisfied and very pleasantly surprised with the outcome of the intra-party talks and accepted Mara's proposal.[35] Issues that had provoked much discussion in the past few years — some form of associated statehood, a

Bahamas-style constitution, a defence arrangement with the United Kingdom, external defence or internal security of an independent Fiji could now be resolved. And to address concerns voiced in the Defence and Overseas Policy Committee about constitutional arrangements that might lead to racial trouble at some future date, steps were taken to ascertain whether the agreement between the two parties was guaranteed. Mara and Koya's invitation for a British minister to visit Fiji was accepted, and Lord Shepherd went out in late January 1970 to obtain 'clear, firm and public statements of their agreement about independence'.[36] Shepherd left London with clear instructions not only about the United Kingdom's refusal to engage in any defence or security arrangement with Fiji, but with the understanding that the United Kingdom would not contribute budgetary aid to an independent Fiji, that development aid with the new nation would have to be renegotiated, that there would be no 'dowry' at independence and, finally, that the British and Fijian governments would share equally in the compensation scheme for permanent and pensionable expatriate officers working for the Government of Fiji.[37]

Shepherd met with a wide cross-section of the community, and especially members of the Council of Chiefs, who reiterated to him familiar and perennial fears and concerns.[38] As expected, the minister found out that the sticking point between the two parties was the method of election. The Alliance was adamantly opposed to the introduction of any form of common roll. The Federation Party presented its case, but Koya had already informed the governor where he stood on the issue. It proposed to Shepherd that they needed more time to study the various proposals the two parties had produced on the composition of the legislature and the method of election. If they were unable to agree on a mutually acceptable formula at the conference, Fiji should contest the first election after independence on a formula approved and settled by the British government. The Alliance readily agreed — as, not surprisingly, did Shepherd.

Shepherd wanted, however, to ensure, in advance, that the Alliance and the Federation parties understood clearly what that formula would be. If 'no agreement was reached and circumstances remained as at present', Shepherd, told the leaders, new, post-independence elections would take place under the provisions of the existing constitution. This, surprisingly, was the same constitution that the Federation Party had rejected and had staged a walkout against in 1967. The death of A. D. Patel, Shepherd noted, was a major factor in the Federation's changed stance. Patel had been steadfast in his commitment to common roll, and would not have accepted a constitution that did not make at least a token movement towards that goal.[39]

The final constitutional conference was held in London in April 1970. Before the leaders gathered, the FCO prepared a series of briefs on issues that were uncontroversial but which still needed to be resolved, such as the status of Rotuman and Banaban people in an independent Fiji, the Commonwealth Sugar Agreement, a general compensation scheme for pensionable expatriate officers employed by the Government of Fiji, defence arrangements and membership of the Commonwealth. The words spoken at the opening session at Marlborough House by both parties alluded to racial harmony, nation-building, a common future, gratitude to the United Kingdom and close links to the Crown, trust, mutual understanding and goodwill.[40] Nineteen sixty-five seemed a distant, faded memory, along with the political turbulence that had accompanied the enactment of the 1965 constitution and marred race relations in the country. Shepherd queried the over-representation of the general voters in Ratu Mara's proposal for the composition of the House of Representatives. Their over-representation, Mara said was a reflection of their preponderant contribution to the economy. He did not mention that general voters always sided with the Fijians.

On common roll, Mara resumed his old tune: common roll was a ruse for Indian domination of Fiji and Fijians would never accept it. 'These fears are like the devil. Many people can prove that there is no devil, yet they are fearful of devils,' he had said on another occasion.[41] The Federation Party presented its case for common roll, and expected Lord Shepherd to impress on the Alliance the need to make at least some token gesture towards accepting it. The Alliance refused — as it had always said it would — and Shepherd, seeking the middle path, proposed that everyone accept common roll as a long-term objective. The Federation Party, in particular its general secretary, K. C. Ramrakha, protested about being misrepresented. The introduction of common roll was their immediate, not long-term, objective. For them to sign a document to that effect would be a betrayal of their party's founding principle. 'Our basic point is that the entire UK delegation proposals rest on the basic misconception that we profess common-roll as a "long-term" objective,' Ramrakha said. 'Since this distorts the entire thinking of the UK delegation, we will call upon you (a) to correct this impression in the plenary session and (b) to submit fresh proposals taking into account the correct viewpoints of the two parties.'[42]

Protest was symbolic, however, although Ramrakha was one of the very few in his party who genuinely believed in the common-roll cause.[43] London and Suva knew where the party leader stood. To break the impasse, Shepherd mooted the idea of a Royal Commission to look into the method of election after independence. Mara and Koya endorsed the proposal, the latter on the understanding, he later claimed, that the recommendations of the commission would be binding — although, as a lawyer, Koya should have known that no independent commission's report can ever be binding for the simple reason that the parliament is supreme. In 1975, a commission was appointed with Professor

Harry Street as chairman, and recommended moving away from a communal roll to a system of proportional representation using the Single Transferable Vote (STV).[44] The Alliance, now firmly in control, refused to consider the report, refused even to have it discussed in parliament. The Federation Party cried foul, but one is left with the lingering suspicion that the Federation leaders, with a few exceptions, did not mind Alliance's about-face on its commitment given at Marlborough House. They had bought the argument that, in view of the declining Indo-Fijian numbers, guaranteed *racial* representation was in their long-term interest. They were encouraged to accept this view by India.[45]

The final constitution was in its most fundamental aspects an extension of the principles and interests that underpinned the 1966 constitution. It preserved the status quo: paramountcy for Fijians, privilege for Europeans and parity for Indo-Fijians. The constitution provided for a bicameral legislature. The Upper House — called the Senate — explicitly recognised the principle of paramountcy. Of its 22 seats, eight were occupied by the nominees of the Council of Chiefs, seven by the nominees of the prime minister, six by the nominees of the leader of the opposition and one by the Council of Rotuma. Given that the prime minister and the leader of the opposition included indigenous Fijians among their nominees, Fijians made up more than half the senate at any given time.

More important than numbers, the nominees of the Council of Chiefs were given the power of veto over all legislation affecting Fijian interests. Section 68 of the independence constitution required the consent of the Council of Chiefs' nominees for the passage of any legislation covering the Fijian Affairs Ordinance, the Native Land Trust Ordinance, the Fijian Development Ordinance, the Rotuma Ordinance, the Agricultural Landlord and Tenant Ordinance, the Banaban Land and Settlement Ordinance and the Rotuma Land Ordinance. In short, Fijian interests were given such watertight protection that no one — apart from Fijian chiefs — could alter or amend legislation pertaining to them.

The lower house — called the House of Representatives — comprised 52 seats, with 22 each for Fijians and Indo-Fijians and eight for general electors (Europeans, part-Europeans, Chinese and 'others'). The principle of parity between Fijians and Indo-Fijians was maintained even though Indo-Fijians made up 50 per cent of the population and Fijians 44 per cent. The principle of European privilege was also maintained. Making up only 4 per cent of the population, the general electors were allocated 15.4 per cent of the seats in the House of Representatives. General elector over-representation was a concern for the United Kingdom, which wanted it reduced substantially, but Mara objected and threatened to resign from public life after returning to Fiji if the United Kingdom persisted. Given the historical association of the general electors with the Fijians, and the record of their political alignment, the Fijians could always count on the general electors for support. In this they were not to be disappointed.

Of the 22 seats each reserved for Fijians and Indo-Fijians, 12 were to be contested on a communal roll and 10 on a national roll — the new name for the old cross-voting seats following the Tanganyika Model. The general electors had eight seats — five national and three communal. The national seats gave advantage to the Fijian and general electors — the Federation Party had not won a single cross-voting seat in the 1966 elections. The logic of the electoral arrangements was clear. If a political party was able to keep its ethnic base intact and split the opposition's, its victory was assured. In this, the Alliance was consistently more successful than the Federation Party.

The logic of the electoral system adopted at independence was that the voters of Fiji would continue to vote on racial lines. A racially based electoral system engendered racial voting, inevitably at the expense of the greater national good. Fiji after independence was not a 'nation' of diverse peoples with common hopes and aspirations but a coalition of competing ethnicities with their own communal agendas. Elections came to be seen not as contests between political parties with competing ideologies, but as zero-sum racial contests. An election lost was thus seen as a loss for a 'race'.

Despite the constitutional obstacles, Fiji experienced social and economic changes in the post-independence era that threatened its political edifice, constructed on the pillars of racial separation.[46] Modern education broadened horizons across the racial divide. Urbanisation and the gradual penetration of the market economy into the hinterland of the country wrought changes in values and expectations. The demands of modern multiracial living in the country's urban centres, the pressures of increasing unemployment and rising costs of living in a fragile economy dependent on global forces were producing new outlooks and habits of thought. Race might have been 'a fact of life', as Ratu Mara said so often, but for many, it was one among many 'facts of life'. The 1970 constitution faced its true test in 1987 when a Fijian party in power for 21 years (from 1966 to 1987) lost the general election to the Fiji Labour Party–National Federation Party Coalition.[47] In the contest between the rhetoric of communalism and the reality on the ground, the rhetoric won. In the South Pacific's first military coup in modern history, an elected government was overthrown, along with the constitution whose formulation had occupied London and Suva for the better part of the 1960s.

Two days before Fiji became independent on 10 October 1970 — exactly 96 years from the date when it had become a British Crown colony — Sir Robert Foster penned his last dispatch as governor of Fiji (Appendix 2). In it, he tried to capture the mood of the moment, the sometimes tumultuous events that had led to it, embroiled it in conflict and tension, and offered his prognosis on what the future held for the young nation.[48] 'Seldom can a country have prepared for independence with such aplomb,' he told London. The diverse people of Fiji, however, 'do not yet seem to think of themselves as a nation', and Julian Amery's fateful word about the difference between the two main communities, written a decade ago, retained some salience. Foster commented on the things that had facilitated the smooth transition to independence: the sobering effects of the 1968 by-elections, the compromising posture of Siddiq Koya and his amicable relations with Mara, a keen appreciation of the realities on the ground — about who controlled the army and the police force, the 'fluffing' of the electoral issue. The future looked reasonably bright: the civil service was professional and apolitical, the security forces efficient and in good morale, and industrial relations were stable. Overall, then, the prospects looked promising.

There were, however, hints of dark clouds over the horizon. The land problem — not ownership but leasing arrangements — remained as intractable as ever. Time had been bought by setting up a committee to examine amendments to the Agricultural Landlord and Tenant Ordinance. 'But a solution to the land problem is no nearer. I doubt whether the problem will ever be solved without far more radical changes in the system of land tenure than Fijians have hitherto been prepared to contemplate.' The second major problem — unresolved at the conference, shelved, to be confronted after independence — was the electoral system.

> A calm search for a just solution to the problem of representation has in the past proved virtually impossible: feelings ran far too deep. One is therefore bound to regret that in effect a time bomb will lie buried in the new Constitution, and to pray that it may be defused before exploding. The two parties have however publicly committed themselves to an act of faith which must give reasonable ground for hope.

Reasonable hope: that, alas, was all that could be hoped for as Fiji took its first tentative steps into an independent future.

ENDNOTES

[1] J. H. Lambert to J. D. B Shaw, 19 July 1968, FCO32/31, on Fiji and the Committee of Twenty-Four.

[2] 'Future of Fiji', Commonwealth Office note of a meeting with Sir R. Foster, 13 August 1968, FCO32/37, no. 18.

[3] Fiji Intelligence Report, CO1036/1216, no. E/91.

[4] Fiji Intelligence Report, CO1036/1216, no. E2/88.

[5] For this assessment, I am grateful to Rod Alley.

[6] Note by G. P. Lloyd, 25 October 1968, FCO32/401, no. 1.

[7] Report on a visit to Fiji by Professor Stanley de Smith, August 1968, FCO32/429.

[8] Letter from Sir D. Jakeway to Sir A. Galsworthy (with enclosures), 12 November 1968, FCO32/401, no. 1

[9] FCO record of a meeting between Ratu Sir K. Mara and Mr Thomson (minister without portfolio), 19 May 1969, FCO32/426.

[10] Quoted in *Fiji Annual Report*, 1968, p. 7.

[11] Electoral arrangements for the Legislative Council of Fiji (enclosure), 19 May 1969, FCO32/426, no. 93.

[12] 'Council of Chiefs', letter from G. P. Lloyd to J. C. Morgan, 15 November 1968, FCO32/401, no. 3.
[13] G. T. P. Marshall to E. J. Emery, 1 May 1969, FCO32/401, no. 81.
[14] Letter from Sir R. Foster to J. C. Morgan, 9 April 1969, FCO32/402, no. 6.
[15] Letter from J. C. Morgan to Sir R. Foster, 2 May 1969, FCO32/402, no. 82.
[16] FCO record of a meeting between Sir A. Galsworthy and Ratu Sir K. Mara, 20 May 1969, FCO32/404.
[17] Letter from J. C. Morgan to Sir R. Foster on Ratu Mara's talks in London, 6 June 1969, FCO32/404, no. 85.
[18] Letter from J. E. Kellick to Ratu Sir K. Mara on the defence of Fijian interests, 11 June 1969, FCO32/426.
[19] A full set of the transcripts is in my possession.
[20] See Mara, Ratu Kamisese 1997, *The Pacific Way: A Memoir*, University of Hawai'i Press, Honolulu, p. 97 (n. 77), where he describes Patel as 'a brilliant lawyer, an eloquent speaker, a charismatic leader of his party, and doughty opponent', but with whom political negotiation had 'proved difficult, and on occasion impossible'.
[21] Rod Alley, who has close knowledge of Fijian politics of the 1960s, says that even if Patel had not died, a settlement was likely, though it would have been different from that achieved with Koya.
[22] I have in my possession a full record of the confidential talks.
[23] Robert Norton (private correspondence) says the idea of an upper house originated in Patel's talks with a prominent Fijian member of the Federation Party, Ratu Julian Toganivalu, who had raised it earlier; but I have not been able to verify this.
[24] Telegram from Sir R. Foster to J. C. Morgan on talks with Ratu Mara, 3 October 1969, FCO32/404, no. 149.
[25] Minute by Sir L. Monson to Lord Shepherd on independence and Fijian paramountcy, 10 October 1969, FCO32/404, no. 154.
[26] 'Fiji Independence', draft memorandum by Mr Stewart for Cabinet Defence and Overseas Policy Committee, 16 October 1969, FCO32/430, no. 154.
[27] Telegram from Sir M. James (New Delhi) to FCO, repeated to Sir R. Foster, 6 November 1969, FCO32/430, no. 74.
[28] FCO records of Sir L. Monson's meetings in Suva with political parties, 29 October – 1 November 1969, FCO32/404, no. 175.
[29] This later helped undermine Koya's stature and influence among his own ranks.
[30] 'Future of Fiji', FCO records of Sir L. Monson's meetings in Suva with Sir R. Foster and Ratu Sir K. Mara, 29 October – 1 November 1969, FCO32/404, no. 175.
[31] By December, Mara had dropped the idea of a defence agreement with the United Kingdom to provide internal security after independence.
[32] Transcript of the inter-party talks, p. 304.
[33] 'Future of Fiji', letter from Sir R. Foster to E. J. Emery, 23 December 1969, FCO32/405, no. 229.
[34] Ibid.
[35] 'Fiji independence', memorandum by Mr Stewart for Cabinet Defence and Overseas Policy Committee, 8 January 1970, FCO32/569, OPD (70), 1.
[36] 'Future of Fiji', minute by H. Steel to E. J. Emery, 13 January 1970, FCO32/580, no. 5.
[37] 'Fiji: independence', Cabinet Defence and Overseas Policy Committee minutes, 16 January 1970, FCO32/569, OPD1 (702), 2.
[38] 'Council of Chiefs', FCO record of a meeting between Lord Shepherd, Ratu Sir K. Mara and the Council of Chiefs, 27 January 1970, FCO32/594, no. 62.
[39] I say this on the basis of my extensive conversations with Patel's closest associates.
[40] Fiji constitutional conference speeches by Lord Shepherd, Ratu Sir K. Mara and Mr Koya, 20 April 1970, FCO32/572, no. 109.
[41] During the inter-party talks in Suva, 94.
[42] Letter from the Federation Party delegation to Lord Shepherd, 28 April 1970, FCO32/582, no. 28.
[43] I base this on my many conversations with him, and from his words on the public record.
[44] Report of a Royal Commission appointed for the purpose of considering and making recommendations as to the most appropriate method of electing members to, and representing the people of Fiji in, the House of Representatives, *Parliamentary Paper*, no. 24/1975.

[45] This is based on my conversations with some of the key figures in Fiji at the time.

[46] For an insightful collection of essays on this subject, see Taylor, Michael (ed.) 1987, *Fiji: Future Imperfect*, Allen and Unwin, Sydney.

[47] An earlier test was 1977 when the Alliance Party temporarily lost power and Mara threatened immediately after the elections that 'blood will flow' if the Indo-Fijians did not respect the deep Fijian attachment to land. See Norton, Robert 1990 (second edn), *Race and Politics in Fiji*, University of Queensland Press, St Lucia, p. 120.

[48] 'Fiji', final dispatch before independence from Sir R. Foster to Sir A. Douglas-Home, 8 October 1970, FCO32/606, no. 1. (Reproduced here as Appendix 2.)

Afterword

The 1970 independence constitution, whose formulation had so exercised the minds of officials in London and Suva during the previous decade, was tested on several occasions and lasted 17 years. It was overthrown in the military coup of 1987. Its overthrow was not a surprise, for the assumptions and understandings that underpinned the constitution, and the political culture of racial compartmentalisation which it had spawned, had been shaken rudely by the social and economic changes sweeping Fiji in the decades after independence.[1]

The first post-independence elections took place in 1972. The Alliance Party, under Ratu Mara's leadership, won easily, capturing 33 seats to the Federation Party's 19. The status quo was maintained. A Fijian party, with a Fijian leader, was at the helm of national leadership, just as the framers of the constitution had envisaged. The two major ethnic groups voted predictably along racial lines, as the race-based electoral system encouraged them to do. The Alliance received 83 per cent of the Fijian communal votes and the Federation Party 75 per cent of the Indo-Fijian votes. Some 2 per cent of Fijians voted for the Federation Party while 24 per cent of Indo-Fijians voted for the Alliance. This was the first and the last time the Alliance would enjoy such encouraging Indo-Fijian support.

As the 1970s progressed, problems began to surface, emanating directly from the racially polarised nature of Fiji's political system. Many Indo-Fijians in the Alliance felt that the party — solidly backed by the Fijians — cared little for their concerns. The government's affirmative action programs in favour of the indigenous community left many disenchanted, as did the dwindling opportunities for Indo-Fijians in the public sector. Some of the formerly staunch Indo-Fijian supporters of the Alliance began to drift towards the National Federation Party. Sections of the Fijian community were also disenchanted with the Alliance government. They felt that the Alliance was unduly pro-Indo-Fijian and favoured the prime minister's own maritime province (Lau) at the expense of other largely neglected areas of Fiji, especially in parts of Viti Levu. They found their champion in Sakiasi Butadroka, formerly of the Alliance, who broke with the party in 1975 to form his own Fijian Nationalist Party, whose founding motto was 'Fiji for the Fijians'.

The politics of moderation under a Fijian leadership, which the Alliance had sought to foster, failed partly because of some of the misconceived policies of the government and partly because of the culture of ethnic polarisation that a racially based electoral system encouraged. Ethnic loyalty rather than secular ideology permeated the thinking of the leaders and the electorate. The first test of the 1970 constitution came in the April 1977 elections. In that election, Butadroka's Nationalist Party won 24 per cent of the Fijian communal votes, enough to cause the downfall of the Alliance, which won 24 seats to the Federation Party's 26. The remaining two went to an independent and to a Nationalist.

The unthinkable had happened. The majority Fijian party, with a high chief as its leader, had lost the elections, while an Indo-Fijian party had 'won'. In fact, strictly speaking, the Federation Party had won exactly half of the 52 seats; to form government, it needed the support of the independents, which was not forthcoming. More seriously, the Federation Party was divided over leadership, over who should be selected to be prime minister. As the party deliberated the issue over several days, the Governor-General, Ratu Sir George Cakobau, 'acting in his own deliberate judgement', appointed Ratu Mara as minority prime minister. He did so, he said, because he had evidence — allegedly from Federation Party sources (who denied any involvement on oath) — that Mara was the leader most likely to command majority support in the House of Representatives. Cakobau's judgement, however, was constitutionally fraught: the issue was for the House of Representatives to decide, not for the Governor-General to pre-empt. He did it anyway, returning Fiji to a Fijian leader, using the Federation Party's delay as his excuse.

The minority Mara government fell shortly afterwards, paving the way for elections in September. The months between the elections restored a sense of 'normalcy' to the political scene. That is, the Alliance re-established its hold on the Fijian constituency. The realisation that splitting the Fijian votes might hand power to an Indo-Fijian party — an anathema at all times — was enough to return many Fijians to the Alliance fold. It won 36 seats and captured 81 per cent of the Fijian communal votes, though only 14 per cent of the Indo-Fijian votes. The Fijian Nationalist Party failed to win a seat. On the other side, the Federation Party fractured into two warring factions — the Dove and the Flower — splitting the Indo-Fijian vote and winning only 15 seats.

The 1977 elections held several lessons for Fiji's political leaders, none more important than the realisation that if the Fijians wanted to retain power, they would have to remain united politically. The lesson was not lost on Mara. According to several of his closest Indo-Fijian colleagues in the Alliance Party, his first priority after the elections was to rally the Fijians behind him and his party, increasingly paying lip-service to the party's multiracial philosophy. Most of the founding Indo-Fijian members of the Alliance began leaving the party to join the Federation Party. The logic of the electoral system reinforced the need for ethnic solidarity in one's own constituency while splitting one's opponents', and leaders of both major parties played the game accordingly. Ethnic divisions were hardening.

Once again, the general elections of 1982 tested the underlying assumptions of the constitution. While the Alliance Party's Indo-Fijian base had slipped considerably, the Federation Party tried to expand its Fijian support, not through direct membership but by forming a coalition with a regional Fijian party, the Western United Front. The final result was close. The Alliance won 28 seats and the Federation Party 24 — a far cry from its form only five years earlier. Both ethnic communities rallied behind their respective parties. The closeness of the anticipated result caused much heat and acrimony, with prophecies of doom for Fijians if the Federation Party ever came to power, endangering their land rights and threatening their other vital interests. Soon after the election, calls went up to reject the 1970 constitution and have it replaced with one that guaranteed Fijian political control in perpetuity, giving the Fijians all the most important portfolios in government.

'Race,' Ratu Mara was fond of saying, '[was] a fact of life in Fiji'. By the late 1970s and early 1980s, however, it had become one among many facts of life in Fiji, and was losing its salience in the daily life of most ordinary citizens. A rapidly expanding cash economy was changing the face of the rural landscape. Urban centres attracted thousands from the countryside; squatter settlements fringed the major towns. Poverty levels increased and the spectre of unemployment began to stalk the country. Travel and technology and a rapidly expanding tertiary education sector were introducing new ideas and values that questioned old habits of thought. The net effect of these developments was the acceleration of social change cutting across the barriers of race. Its political manifestation was the formation, in 1985, of a multiracial Fiji Labour Party (FLP) headed by Dr Timoci Bavadra. Two years later, it teamed up with the Federation Party to contest the 1987 general elections; a fateful decision, as it transpired, because it signalled to Fijian nationalists that the FLP was 'on the same side' as the overwhelmingly Indo-Fijian Federation Party. The Coalition ended the Alliance Party's 21-year reign by winning 28 seats in the 52-seat House of Representatives.

The elections also disrupted the conventional calculus of Fijian politics. A Fijian-dominated party, representing the Fijian establishment, was defeated. The number of Fijians voting for the Coalition was small, fewer than 10 per cent; 77 per cent of the Fijians voted for the Alliance, and 83 per cent of Indo-Fijians for the National Federation Party. The shift was slight, but the fear of the spreading of the trend of non-racial voting challenged conventional thinking about the operation of politics in Fiji. Fijians used to seeing their high chiefs at the helm of national leadership were reluctant to accept the new government even though it was headed by an indigenous Fijian, albeit of a less-exalted status than his predecessor. Politicians piqued by loss of office manipulated the fears of the ethnic Fijians to derail the new government. A month later, on 14 May, the Coalition government was overthrown in a military coup led by Sitiveni Rabuka.

An interim administration ruled the country from 1987 to 1992. One of its principal tasks was to devise a new constitution to replace the abrogated 1970 constitution. The new constitution it recommended removed multiracial voting altogether, taking the country back two decades. Of the 71 seats in the proposed House of Representatives, 37 were allocated to Fijians, 27 to Indo-Fijians and the remainder to 'others'. Of the 37 Fijian seats, 32 were to be contested from rural constituencies and only five from urban ones even though, by the early 1990s, more than 40 per cent of the indigenous Fijians lived in urban areas. The framers of the constitution hoped that the electoral arrangements would reinforce ethnic Fijian solidarity, the slippage of which had cost Fijians the national leadership. The urban Fijians who had voted for Labour were marginalised in the new electoral arrangement.

To promote Fijian political unity, the Great Council of Chiefs launched an exclusively Fijian party, the *Soqosoqo Vakavulewa ni Taukei* (SVT) in 1992, as an umbrella organisation for Fijians of all political persuasions. Predictably, the hope of ethnic unity was short lived. The first tensions erupted over the leadership of the party. Some Fijians preferred a high chief as leader to give the new organisation authority and prestige, while others wanted a secret ballot to decide who the leader should be. Rabuka, who was not a chief, won the presidency of the party handily, much to the disappointment of the more traditional members of the establishment who soon afterwards broke away to form their own political party, the Fijian Association Party, with the support of Ratu Mara, whose dismissive attitude to Rabuka was public knowledge. Rabuka's Fijian opponents brought about his government's defeat on the floor of the House in 1994, but he won government in the elections that followed and remained prime minister until 1999.

By then it was abundantly clear that Fijian political unity was an evanescent dream. Later in the decade, political fragmentation was the most prominent feature of indigenous Fijian politics. Class and regional calculations came to the fore. The departure from the national scene of paramount chiefs — who had wielded unquestioned political power in the postwar period — opened up space for other aspirants. The substantial decline of the Indo-Fijian population after the 1987 coups lessened the fear of 'Indian domination', which had been an important factor in forging Fijian political unity. By the late 1990s, the political and intellectual underpinnings of the 1970 constitution were demonstrably irrelevant.

It was in the midst of all these changes and transformations that the Fiji Constitution Review Commission was appointed by parliament to review the contested 1990 constitution, in accordance with the provision for a review seven years after its promulgation. Two fundamental questions — which had long plagued Fiji — confronted the commission as it began its task. One was how best to protect the interests of the Fijian community, or the 'paramountcy of Fijian interests'. The second was how to enlarge the space in the political system for non-racial politics. The commission recommended that the Great Council of Chiefs be recognised in the constitution, complete with its own secretariat to help protect its independence and autonomy. Further, all the legislative provisions pertaining to Fijian interests — land ownership, customary titles and so on — should continue to be guaranteed. In short, matters of deep concern to the indigenous community should be removed from the arena of electoral politics. Regarding the promotion of non-racial democracy, the commission recommended that Fiji should move away gradually but decisively from a race-based electoral system. Forty-six of 71 seats should be contested on open, non-racial rolls and the remaining on a racially allocated basis though only for a temporary period. The way forward for Fiji, the commission believed, was through genuine multi-ethnic cooperation rather than through ethnic compartmentalisation.

The Parliamentary Select Committee appointed to scrutinise the report of the Fiji Constitution Review Commission and make the final recommendations to the parliament for a new constitution reversed the commission's electoral recommendations. It recommended that 46 seats should be racially reserved for the three communities indefinitely, and the remaining 25 seats contested on a non-racial basis. The parliament that approved the final constitution comprised members elected on racial rolls prescribed by the 1990 constitution. Having entered parliament through a racially segregated electoral system, and having spent their entire careers in racially compartmentalised politics, members of parliament resisted taking the bold step in the direction of non-racialism that the commission recommended. The 25 open seats were a start, but the 46 racially reserved seats meant that Fiji was still tethered to its racial past. There was one ameliorating feature of the constitution that sought to mitigate the deleterious effects of ethnically polarised politics. It was the provision that any political party with more than 10 per cent of seats in the House of Representatives — that is, eight or more members — was constitutionally entitled to be invited to serve in cabinet. The route to parliament was, however, still through a dominantly racial electoral system.

When Mahendra Chaudhry's Labour-led People's Coalition won the 1999 elections, the Fijian nationalists once again played the race card against an 'Indian-dominated' government. The coup that overthrew this government on 19 May 2000 was essentially about the distribution of power within the indigenous community, but race was mobilised to depose the government. Every legislative agenda the government proposed — from land use to its forest policy — was viewed and assessed through a racial lens. Racial prejudice fostered by a racial electoral system over the decades came to the fore and was manipulated to the full by the supporters of the coup. Chaudhry defended his government on the basis that it had a mandate from the people, given to it through a democratic election. The government did not, however, have a mandate from the Fijian people, the majority of whom voted for Fijian parties. Race remained central, too, in the elections of 2001, which followed the intervention of the army and the installation of an interim government under Prime Minister Laisenia Qarase. His new party, the *Soqosoqo Duavata ni Lewenivanua* (SDL), was dedicated to unifying indigenous Fijians, and he received their overwhelming support at the ballot box — enough to keep him in power for the next five years with a policy aimed at favouring the indigenous population at the expense of the Indo-Fijians.

The 2006 general elections produced a result that would have pleased officials at the 1960s Colonial Office. A democratically elected government, with an indigenous Fijian at its head, was in power under a constitution supported widely throughout the community. Even more, for the first time in Fiji's history, a genuinely multi-ethnic government was in place, thanks to the power-sharing provision of the constitution. With the Fijian population nearing 60 per cent and the Indo-Fijian population about 37 per cent, Fijian fears of Indian domination were diminishing. A demographic transition was finally producing the result that had preoccupied policy makers in Suva and London for so long.

Just when 'victory' seemed within sight, however, Commodore Frank Bainimarama executed Fiji's fourth coup and removed Qarase's SDL government from power. For the first time, neither race nor the protection of Fijian rights were at issue in a Fijian coup; the removal of a government reported to be riddled with corruption and variously patronising individuals implicated in George Speight's coup was advertised as the key reason. The military-backed Interim Administration is intent on remaining in power for some time. One of its stated intentions is to review the constitution to remove all vestiges of racial voting. If it succeeds, it will have executed a fundamental constitutional revolution; but it is too early to tell either whether this goal will be achieved or what the outcome of doing so will be.

The role of traditional Fijian institutions in the public life of Fiji — in particular that of the Great Council of Chiefs — was a major preoccupation of the policy makers in Suva and London on the eve of independence. In the 1970 constitution, the Great Council of Chiefs was given the power of veto over all legislation that even remotely affected Fijian interests and concerns. After independence, the Great Council of Chiefs continued to be consulted on issues of importance not only to the indigenous community but to the nation as a whole. Its voice carried weight. The 1997 constitution recognised the Great Council of Chiefs as a constitutional entity in the expectation that it would become the guardian of the national interest as well. After the 2006 coup, however, the Great Council of Chiefs was humiliated symbolically by the military when it was rudely sidelined and silenced. Its membership was suspended when it refused to endorse the military's nominee for vice-president. The military wants a much narrower social and cultural role for the Great Council of Chiefs, chiefly as a voice of the indigenous community, and not much more. If it succeeds in its efforts to redefine a subordinate national role for the Great Council of Chiefs, the military will have executed yet another coup of far-reaching significance for Fijian public life.

The issues that preoccupied decision makers in London and Suva in the 1960s continued to haunt Fiji in its post-independence years. The entrenchment of a racial system of voting — which the Fijians and Europeans demanded, almost as a precondition for further moves towards internal self-government and eventually independence, and which the Colonial Office endorsed, albeit reluctantly — in time became the principal cause of Fiji's political problems, derailing its fragile democracy. A time bomb did indeed lie buried at the heart of Fiji's independence constitution.

ENDNOTES

[1] Since this is a small survey, I thought it unnecessary to have it documented like the rest of the text. For readers seeking more details of the picture portrayed here, I refer them to my published and easily accessible works: *Broken Waves: A history of the Fiji Islands in the 20th century* (1992), *Another Way: The politics of constitutional reform in post-coup Fiji* (1997) and *Islands of Turmoil: Elections and politics in Fiji* (2006).

Appendix 1. Policy in Fiji (Nov. 1960)
By
Julian Amery
Parliamentary Undersecretary of State
At the Colonial Office, 1958–60

1. The Fijians and Indians are more distinct as communities than Jews and Arabs in Palestine, Greeks and Turks in Cyprus or even Europeans and Bantu in South and Central Africa. Intermarriage, business associations, even personal friendships are rare.

2. In the past, so long as we have held the undisputed power, relations between the communities have been good if distant. In the past few months this has changed. The December riots and sugar dispute have made the Fijians fear that the Indians are out to bring the wind of change to Fiji and use it to establish Indian preponderance. Their fears have been further increased by the Burns report which they regard as an attempt to give the Indian community control of the land by breaking up traditional Fijian society. The resentment aroused by the Burns report has been to some degree extended to Government and for the first time for many years, has shaken Fijian confidence in British intentions. The point is crucial when it is remembered that the Fijians are the 'loyal' community providing 75 per cent of the security forces. The Islands could hardly be governed without them, let alone against them.

3. In this climate the Fijians have become increasingly communally minded. They have also become more resistant than before both to constitutional changes for the Colony as a whole and to the modification of their own traditional system. In the face of what they regard as the Indian threat, there has been an instinctive closing of the ranks around their traditional Chiefs.

4. The Indians on their side are sharply divided over the sugar issue and over the proper course to follow in their relations with the Fijians. The more moderate leaders among them realise that they have antagonized the Fijians and would like to heal the breach. At the same time they are subject to fairly strong pressures from within their own community; and the more extreme elements are thinking in terms of self-government on the basis of a common roll which would enable the Indo-Fijians to rule the roost.

5. How then should we proceed in the constitutional field and in regard to the Burns recommendations about Fijian administration?

6. To begin with, we must, I think, accept that it is impracticable to think in terms of a single Fijian nation or of a common roll at any rate for the foreseeable future. Any suggestion of this is bound to arouse Fijian suspicions that the Indians would dominate by counting heads. The moderate Indian leaders recognize this. This points to the conclusion that we will have to recognize not

just the equality of individuals before the law but the equality of Indian and Fijian communities irrespective of their numbers. There is no other way of reconciling both the pledges in the Deed of Cession and those in Lord Salisbury's dispatch, let alone the need to keep communal peace. We should, therefore, let it be known that any constitutional advance must be so designed as to preclude the domination of the two main communities by the other.

7. The European community (20,000) can hardly expect, in the long run, to maintain their position as a community equal in importance to Fijians and Indians. For the time being, however, the Fijians insist that they should be so regarded. The Indians for their part have not asked for any change in the status of the European community.

Leg. Co. and Ex. Co.

8. The Indians have asked, but not pressed, for an official majority on Leg. Co and Ex. Co. while preserving the present communal composition of both. The Fijians are flatly opposed to any reduction in the Governor's powers.

9. After full discussion with the Governor and his advisors we came to the conclusion that the best way to proceed would be to reverse the traditional colonial pattern and introduce a quasi-ministerial system while observing the official majority in the Leg. Co. The 'Ministers' who would be bound by the ordinary doctrine of collective responsibility, would count as officials for the purpose of securing the official majority. They would of course be dismissed and replaced by others if they ceased to support the Governor. Leg. Co itself would be somewhat expanded, though on a communal basis, to balance the expansion of Ex. Co. resulting from the introduction of the Ministerial system. The composition of Ex. Co. would not be laid down, so that, if all members of the community refused in certain circumstances to serve, the governor could still govern with the help of the other two communities and his officials.

10. A change of this kind is likely to be criticised by A. D. Patel and those Indians who consider that their numbers entitle them to a predominant position. The Governor and his advisers, however believe that the 'jobs' created by the introduction of a ministerial system will be popular with leading men in both communities and that there will be little difficulty in maintaining the official majority in Leg. Co. They consider that such a system might work for a number of years.

11. If this general principle is accepted, its implementation might be carried out in two phases. In the first, the Governor would simply invite existing members of Ex. Co. to assume ministerial functions on a basis of collective responsibility. In the second, and only after the next election, the number of seats in Leg. Co. would be increased.

The Public Service

12. Just as the Fijians will not accept a common roll, so they will not accept that recruitment for the public service should be solely on a basis of merit regardless of race. The Indians are probably abler and certainly have more graduates than the Fijians. On this basis they would soon dominate the Administration. This the Fijians will not accept. In the long run, it will probably be necessary to have some rule — as in Cyprus now or in India in the old days — under which government jobs would be divided in some such proportion as Indians 45 per cent, Fijians 45 per cent, Europeans and others 10 per cent in each grade of each department. For the time being there is no need to be so precise and we can probably continue on the present basis on promotion according to merit subject to a public assurance that neither community will get more than 45 per cent of the jobs in any grade or department. It will be some time before the Fijians can hope to provide suitable candidates to fill their quota and meanwhile Europeans will have to fill their places. Later on it will from time to time become necessary as good Fijians come forward to pass over Europeans who are marginally better qualified. This will raise problems of compensation and it is for consideration how far these would be covered under the terms of the new White Paper as applied in Fiji.

The Fijian Administration

13. I see no future in the Burns recommendation that the Fijian administration should be wound up as soon as possible. The Fijians are determined to resist any move in this direction. They realise that whatever its defects the tribal system does provide a leadership capable of defending the Fijian communal interest against what they regard as the Indo-Fijian threat. Without their chiefs they would be leaderless. In many respects, of course, the Fijian administration is old fashioned and we should seek opportunities of modernizing it. But rather than curtail its activities I would be inclined to give it more responsibilities particularly in the sphere of local government. It may still be possible to develop multi-racial local government except in a second tier (i.e. delegations of Fijian and Indo-Fijian local government bodies meeting in joint conference). In each case the Fijian Administration could play a big part.

14. I would personally be inclined to go further and encourage the development of some Indian counterpart to the Fijian administration. This would offer Indians opportunities for public service which they both want and need. The existence of two communal organizations moreover would help us to overcome a major problem. At the present time, many necessary development or administrative projects tend by their nature to favour one community rather than the other. Fair shares for all is a slogan which makes government hesitate to do anything for anybody. If roughly equal subsidies could be given to both communities to spend as each thought best there would be less cause for jealousy. Scholarships

are a case in point. A number of Indian children are educated abroad at their parents' expense. Few Fijians can afford this. The Fijians are thus keener on scholarships than the Indians. Yet at present scholarships which are centrally administrated have to be given on a basis of merit; and the Indo-Fijians — deservedly on this basis — tend to scoop the pool. If scholarships were a communal matter, the Fijians would probably spend more on them than would the Indians who could then spend the money on other projects of which they are in greater need.

15. Hitherto we have held up the concept of a single multi-racial community as the goal towards which Fijians and Indians alike should strive. The Fijians will no longer accept this; and the more we lay the emphasis on multi-racialism, the more suspicious they will become that we plan to sell them out to the Indians. The only way, in my view, to exorcise the fear of communal domination is to make it clear 'as of now' that we stand for equal rights for both communities as communities and that we shall not pull out until both ask us to do so.

Appendix 2. Fiji Final Dispatch (8 Oct. 1970)
By
Sir Robert Foster
Governor of Fiji

It is hard to believe that in two days' time Fiji's new flag will rise slowly to the top of the mast in the presence of His Royal Highness The Prince of Wales and distinguished representatives of foreign powers. For seldom can a country have prepared for independence with such aplomb; there has been an air of quiet satisfaction and polite interest during the last few months, but no sign of the nationalistic braggadocio which one has grown to expect. This is not to say that the prospect is not widely welcomed. It most certainly is. But the diverse people of these islands do not yet seem to think of themselves as a nation, and reserve their fervour for the rugby and soccer fields.

2. Ten years ago Mr Julian Amery wrote

> The Fijians and Indians are more distinct as communities than Jews and Arabs in Palestine, Greeks and Turks in Cyprus, or Europeans and Bantu in South and Central Africa. Intermarriage, business associations, even personal friendships are rare.

3. There remains some truth in his judgment. But whereas in the past relations were dominated by a mixture of fear and suspicion, today this has been replaced by a frank acknowledgment that potentially dangerous differences exist and a widespread acceptance that only by playing it cool can Fiji avoid following Malaysia to the very edge of the pit.

4. No one appreciates this better than the leaders of the two major political parties, Ratu Sir Kamisese Mara (Alliance) and Mr S. M. Koya (National Federation), who themselves could hardly be more different in character or appearance. Mara is a six foot four aristocrat, the *Tui Nayau*, paramount chief of Lau, the eastern group of Fiji's islands; a dignified and most impressive figure. Koya is a plump little lawyer, full of intrigue and calculation, who wears a mask of amiable geniality which occasionally slips to reveal the hatchet man beneath.

5. Mara, however, is very far from being a typical Fijian. He was the first of his race ever to become an MA and prior to this completed five years' medical training in New Zealand. He also has a diploma in economics from LSE. He is a man of vision who sincerely believes that, with tolerance and understanding, each community can retain its own identity whilst at the same time contributing to make Fiji into a nation; and he is not afraid to pursue policies to this end, even if they entail sacrifices not popular with his people. But he also believes (without being anti-Indian) that Fijian-paramountcy is proper and natural, if

only because his race would not tolerate any alternative so that an attempt to impose one would inevitably provoke violence. Personally a moody, shy and solitary man who inspires awe rather than confidence, he nevertheless has a keen sense of humour and is capable of exercising very great charm when in a relaxed mood. But unfortunately he reverts under pressure to a dictatorial arrogance which does not make him easy to work with. One result of this is that his Ministers are frightened of him, so that too little authority has been delegated and decisions are often slow in coming. Some of the younger members of his party have fretted against the bit in the past, but since the London Conference there have been no signs of the upsets in the party which had previously given rise to cause for concern.

6. Nor is Koya a typical Indian. For a start he is a Muslim in a predominately Hindu party, of which he became the leader about a year ago on the death of Mr A. D. Patel who had led it since its formation. He is a very different man to his predecessor: Patel was born in India, learned his politics there and came to Fiji as a mature adult with beliefs already hardened. He never shook off (or grew out of) many of the attitudes of the Congress leaders of the early nineteen twenties, although most of these have long been outmoded. He was an intellectual, sincere and dedicated, but misguided. His opponents respected some of his qualities no matter how bitterly they disliked his views, but they never trusted him very far. Koya on the other hand was born in Fiji and is very much a man of this country. Unlike Patel he has a distinctly murky past, having over a number of years been closely involved with a well known bunch of murderers and thugs whom he defended in court whenever they slipped up and secretly advised outside. Before he became leader of the party he had not been noted for his moderation and had never missed an opportunity to exploit anti-European feeling. But he has never shared Patel's main fault as a politician — a complete inability to compromise. A wheeler-dealer if ever there was one, he probably has no basic principles.

7. These then are the two men who have presided over the two major parties during the last year. They share an interest in power and a distaste for colonialism, being sufficiently political animals to operate on the same wavelength. More indeed than that, they have achieved a remarkable degree of mutual trust and accord which has facilitated inter-party agreement and even led some to speculate about the chances of a coalition Government. Although sure that Koya would dearly like to become a minister, I doubt whether this is a serious possibility for several years. But before hazarding guesses as to what the future may hold, I should perhaps turn to what has happened since my predecessor's dispatch of the 11th January 1968, written when the Opposition was boycotting the Legislative Council, and by-elections in the nine Indian communal constituencies seemed likely to result: for during this period Fiji has, politically speaking, been turned upside down and will never be the same again.

8. By-elections duly became necessary after the Opposition did not appear at two consecutive meetings. They took place in the autumn of 1968 and were preceded by a bitter campaign vigorously conducted by both parties. The Alliance by then had over 30,000 Indian members on their books and had convinced themselves that they stood a real chance of winning a large measure of Indian support. They thus confidently expected to reduce the majorities in most, if not all, constituencies and even to win one or two seats.

9. This was not however to be. The results were little short of a landslide. All nine National Federation Party candidates were successful and most received an increased share of the poll. Despite the earlier assurances which they had received, the Alliance only managed to attract a total of 12,000 votes (this was nevertheless 20 per cent of the poll and proof of not unsubstantial Indian support — far more than the NFP would obtain from Fijians).

10. Fijians then felt that their leaders had extended the hand of friendship to the Indians only to have it brushed aside, and that promises had not been kept. Moreover they were angry that during the campaign abuse had been heaped upon Mara, and indirectly on his fellow chiefs. The outcome was a highly emotional reaction. There ensued a round of Fijian Association meetings held in all the main centres at which were passed some extreme resolutions, often verging on the seditious. One group of warriors marched through the streets daubed in war paint. Another processed with a banner saying 'Kill the Indians'. For a couple of months there was an ugly atmosphere almost throughout the country. Mara and his colleagues, every bit as disappointed and bitter as their supporters at what, with some justification, they regarded as a cynical rejection of their very genuine and sincere overtures, at first made no effort to restrain their people. It was only after repeated stone-throwing incidents and assaults by Fijians on Indians that he was prevailed upon to produce a very lukewarm statement, calling the hounds off. Although he was at once obeyed he had by then allowed the Fijian back-lash to progress almost to the brink: there could easily have been widespread and potentially serious disorder.

11. As a result of all this, the political situation changed fundamentally. On the one hand the Alliance, hitherto disinclined to consider early constitutional change started to do some hard thinking. Mara appointed a research group of well educated young Fijians for the purpose. Both they and he himself soon concluded that the best policy would be to go for early independence whilst the country was still under Fijian leadership. At about this time Ratu Penaia Ganilau, then Minister for Fijian Affairs and Local Government as a civil servant and now shortly to be appointed a Senator and to become Deputy Prime Minister and Minister for Defence, observed with unaccustomed vehemence at a Fijian Intelligence Committee meeting that the Fijians had now come to see clearly

where they stood and had realised that they must take the initiative if they were to remain in their own house.

12. On the other hand the Opposition was thoroughly alarmed. Ordinary Indian country folk were apprehensive about their own and their families' safety, whilst businessmen foresaw damage to property and looting. The party's triumph at the polls was therefore so short lived that it could really be called still-born. They immediately dropped all activities which Fijians might consider provocative. In addition they became extremely cooperative in Legislative Council, doing all in their power to heal the breach. And they began to say they wanted to hold private talks with the Alliance about constitutional change, with a view to there being another conference if these succeeded. Mara soon responded if at first with some suspicion and only because it suited what by then had become his book as well as theirs. After some initial sparring and many delays, one caused by the illness and death of Patel which in fact opened the way for progress, the two parties eventually got down to serious discussion. Early last November they announced their wish that the next move should be to what they then called 'Dominion status'. A month later Mara informed me that they had reached agreement that Fiji should proceed to this stage without further elections and as quickly as possible.

13. From then on events have moved at what has often seemed a bewildering pace. In January this year Lord Shepherd visited Fiji. He formed the opinion that, despite continuing differences of view over the key question of electoral arrangements, accord might be reached before or during a Constitutional Conference. One was duly held in London during April. It was a success, and very shortly, on the 10th October, the ninety-sixth anniversary of Cession, Fiji will become an independent member of the Commonwealth.

14. That so much has been achieved can be a matter of satisfaction for all concerned. To achieve it, however, the electoral issue had to be fluffed. For 'having regard to the national good and for peace, order and good government of independent Fiji' the Conference settled on an interim composition for the new House of Representatives. It went on to record agreement;

> that at some time after the next general election and before the second election the Prime Minister, after consultation with the Leader of the Opposition, should arrange that a Royal Commission should be set up to study and make recommendations for the most appropriate method of election and representation for Fiji and that the terms of reference should be agreed by the Prime Minister with the Leader of the Opposition ... Parliament would, after considering the Royal Commission Report, provide through Legislation for the composition and method of election of a new House of Representatives, and ... such legislation so passed would be regarded as an entrenched part of the Constitution.

15. A calm search for a just solution to the problem of representation has in the past proved virtually impossible; feelings ran too deep. One is therefore bound to regret that in effect a time bomb will lie buried in the new Constitution, and to pray it may be defused before exploding. The two parties have however, publicly committed themselves to an act of faith which must give reasonable ground for hope.

16. There are other grounds for this too: the new nation will start with many advantages. The economy is healthy. As developing countries go it is not badly off. There are few really poor people in Fiji, nor are there many millionaires. The average *per capita* income is about £150.0.0. Food is plentiful and, by and large, so is water. Much of the land could be more intensively farmed. An enlightened family planning program, unopposed by any religious group, has succeeded in reducing the birthrate from 40.88 per thousand in 1961 to 28.97 per thousand in 1969. The standard of medical services is relatively high. Ninety-five per cent of children of primary school age attend school. There are admirable traditions of voluntary public service and of self-help.

17. The Civil Service is efficient, remarkably free from corruption and generally apolitical. The Independence Constitution contains the standard provisions to safeguard against patronage, and although there are already signs that Mara and Koya may find these irksome I am hopeful that the worst abuse of a spoils system will be avoided. Localization has proceeded at what some regard as a dangerously rapid pace, but is not likely to result in the traumatic experiences from which many countries have suffered. For one thing, there is a widespread recognition that an important handful of top administrators and key professional officers will be needed for some time: it is indicative of this that Mara has told the present expatriate Secretary to the Council of Ministers, who will be the first Secretary to the Cabinet, thus he can look forward to staying here for at least five years. For another, almost three quarters of the overseas officers in Fiji are on contract or on secondment, so that there is no question of their being compensated and retiring prematurely. And finally, the country is fortunate enough to possess a substantial number of senior local officers with good qualifications and reasonable ability.

18. Industrial relations have been remarkably stable during the last couple of years. The Trade Union movement is led by moderate, sensible men; and employers, by and large, have behaved in a reasonable fashion. The two Union leaders who caused serious trouble in the past have been away in Australia for some time. Both are ostensibly studying, one at The Australian National University for a PhD and the other no one knows quite what, under the tutelage of Dr Cairns, the leading figure on the left wing of the Australian Labor Party.

19. The country's isolated position in the middle of the enormous Pacific is in one sense an asset; it is shielded to a very great extent from the influence of

external ideologies and events. Although a few individuals have been exposed to communist parties and individuals overseas there is no present likelihood of the ideology itself being introduced. There are no incipient revolutionary bodies nor are there any primitive cults. There is no history of serious riots and civil commotion and there is no present subversion. Even slogans like 'Black Power', 'Student Power', 'the New Left', etc. are virtually unknown, although the recent foundation of the University of the South Pacific may change this. Some of the lecturers there certainly appear anxious to encourage dissent.

20. The Fiji Military Forces and the Police are efficient, and their morale is high. But the loss of UK backup in the event of serious disorder will leave a yawning gap. Plans have accordingly been made to create a Police Mobile force, especially trained in riot duties, and to enlarge the FMF, giving them more modern IS training and equipment. Implementing these may however cost more than the country can rapidly afford, and it is to be hoped that generous assistance will be forthcoming.

21. This is not to say that there are no serious problems: indeed the most immediate one concerns the future of the sugar industry, which still forms the backbone of Fiji's economy and provides a livelihood for 15,000 peasant growers.

22. Late last year Lord Denning, the Master of the Rolls, arbitrated in a dispute between these growers and the sugar millers, South Pacific Sugar Mills Ltd., an almost wholly-owned subsidiary of the Australian Colonial Sugar Refining Company Ltd Rightly judging that the Company had done well over a substantial period, he decided to tip the scales in the growers' favour. Whether he tipped them too far is a matter of opinion. The Company obviously thought so. After a long silence it pressed Government privately to decide at once to buy its assets on terms to be settled, saying it would then be prepared to continue running the mills and marketing sugar for a period, on a fee basis.

23. The pressure proved counterproductive. Even had Ministers thought that its offer was attractive, they could not for political reasons have afforded to give the appearance of being the Company's puppets. On the contrary, they were determined to show the public that it would be obliged to dance to their tune. For it has long been regarded by local people as at best paternalistic and all too often a bully, browbeating the Fiji Government into helping it make assured profits at the growers' expense and not above a bit of trickery in the process. As a result both the Alliance and the NFP had engaged counsel to support the growers against it during the arbitration. Both had subsequently claimed credit for the favourable decision, being thus committed to making the Company accept this.

24. Having realized it must adjust its tactics the Company then published a critique of the award, purporting to prove that it could not operate profitably under the proposed new contract. The following day it announced that it would

nevertheless sign this, but, more in sorrow than in anger, would give notice in accordance with the law to withdraw from operation in Fiji after the next three seasons.

25. It may secretly have been glad of a good excuse to disengage. Accustomed to count on Government support, it was plainly going to face suspicion and perhaps hostility: a position long privileged had of a sudden become uncomfortably vulnerable. In Australia it has anyway been busily diversifying out of sugar, which is not a good long term prospect. Moreover almost half the sugar which Fiji produces has hitherto been sold to the UK at favourable prices under the Commonwealth Sugar Agreement. But for this assured market the industry would not have been viable; and the market is now at risk as a result of the UK's application to join the EEC.

26. However all that may be, Government was obliged to declare its firm intention that the mills would continue to operate after 1972 and that SGSM might have to be purchased 'for the people of Fiji'. Having done so, it had to face complex questions about future ownership, management and marketing. Advice on possible answers to some of these has already been provided by a UK firm of Chartered Accountants, one of whose senior partners visited here under Technical Assistance arrangements. And a Select Committee of Legislative Council has opened discussions with CSR. It includes members of both parties, for this is rightly regarded as a national issue. The discussions are certain to be protracted and tough, but there seems a reasonable chance that they can be successfully concluded, without bitterness.

27. From the country's point of view their timing is nevertheless unfortunate, for if its biggest overseas investor is seen to be pulling out on independence, hazarding the future of its most important industry, the appearance must be given that there may be good cause for anxiety about political instability, or about nationalization. There is not yet any sign of a consequential loss of business confidence, though the risk must be obvious.

28. Though sugar poses the most immediate problem, race relations may prove the most perplexing. I do not imply that the atmosphere is ordinarily tense: far from it. Despite the fundamental and abiding differences between them, the two major communities here co-exist in a quite surprisingly relaxed manner. There are nevertheless many sensitive subjects. Each needs to be handled with particular care, for fear of arousing the sort of angry passions which can drive men to senseless violence.

29. One such subject is land. Of this there is not by the standards of many other countries a real shortage. But a lot of people here think there is, and this colours their attitudes. Moreover most of the parts which are suited to intensive agriculture have of course already been developed; and Indians occupy a large proportion of them and prosper accordingly, although Fijians own 83 per cent

of the country's land area. So the Fijians, not by nature hard-working peasant farmers and not in the past anxious to change their ways, now feel they have somehow been cheated of opportunities they would like. They are in consequence increasingly determined to recover the use of the better agricultural areas. Meanwhile the Indians feel with some justice that in the national interest all land should be properly used, and they look covetously at Fijian Reserves which too often appear neglected.

30. The Agricultural Landlord and Tenant Ordinance was enacted in 1966 and brought into force the following year in the hope of containing the situation equitably enough to satisfy all concerned. It provided tenants with a right to renew their leases if they could prove greater hardship than their landlords, and with an entitlement to compensation for improvements if dispossessed. As a *quid pro quo* it also made provision for landlords to revise rents upwards, to 6 per cent of the market value of their land. Revision took some time to arrange however, so the Fijians were slow to appreciate the potential value of the Ordinance and it came under heavy fire after the 1968 by-elections. Its repeal was only averted by some skilful manoeuvering by Mara himself, which involved setting up a Committee to consider amendments to it. During the past year or so many Fijians appear to have realized that its basic principles are fairer than they had at first thought. With the apparent concurrence of both sides of the House, the Committee has therefore avoided reaching any conclusions yet. As a result the Ordinance will now be enshrined in the new Constitution — so amendments will require the approval of two-thirds of both Houses of Parliament.

31. Further time has been bought in this way. But a solution to the land problem is no nearer. I doubt whether the problem will ever be solved without far more radical changes in the system of land tenure than Fijians have hitherto been prepared to contemplate. Any attempt to impose such changes would provoke a thoroughly hostile reaction; unless they commanded popular confidence they would stand no chance of success. There are however now some signs that people are at least beginning to question the present paternalistic arrangements. These vest control of Fijian land in the Native Land Trust Board, a body which is hopelessly inefficient and probably corrupt. It has the power to negotiate leases without consulting the landowners, and it deducts 25 per cent of all rents for its services. Once a sacred cow, it is fast becoming an Aunt Sally. An increasing number of Fijians favour drastic reform. They feel, with justification, that they are no longer children, that land is their only capital (of which they are chronically short) and that they ought to be permitted greater powers of decision. Few may yet be prepared to contemplate any substantial lifting of the restrictions on the alienation of their land; but it is significant that a question long taboo can now be discussed.

32. Another sensitive subject is the racial composition of the Civil Service. Fijians still outnumber Indians in it, though the better qualifications and greater diligence of the latter win them more of the senior positions. Hitherto, as a generalization, the Service has in consequence been officered by expatriates, and has had Indians NCOs and Fijian privates. If rapid localization were to result in Indo-Fijian officers as well as NCOs much bitterness might result. Except for lawyers the most outstanding locals are by chance a mixed bunch, so the top managerial posts are likely to be equitably distributed. Moreover it has proved possible to distinguish the areas (like the Administration) where undue imbalance might result in a public outcry, and to ensure that particular attention is paid to the staffing of these. However the Judicial and Legal Departments are vulnerable areas and will continue to be so for a few years.

33. Yet another sensitive subject is that of employment generally. When jobs are scarce, members of each community are always liable to resent losing an opportunity of work to someone of another race. Fijians also now realize how much they have missed by failing to start businesses of their own. Their reaction is to blame everyone else for their lack of the necessary capital and training, and to ignore the fact that with greater effort and resolution they could have done much to help themselves. A reconstituted and (hopefully) revitalized Ministry of Fijian Affairs is to be charged with particular responsibility for securing for them a fairer slice of the economic cake, probably by providing them with special assistance.

34. The Government recognizes that this alone will not suffice: the essential is that Fijians' dismal performance in school examinations should be improved, so they become better qualified to compete on equal terms in an aggressive world. An Education Advisory Committee reported last year, making recommendations designed to give them preferential treatment with this object in view. Perhaps more important still is the recognition by Fijian leaders that success must ultimately depend on the efforts made by children of their own race. If they can get this message across to parents, the effect may be dramatic.

35. Many of the measures I have mentioned must seem to be designed to accord Fijians privileges which others will be denied. They are; and are probably necessary. For racial inequalities are at the root of all the problems under discussion. The Fijian people have a growing awareness of the present differences between their wealth and opportunity and that of other races. They may as a result become embittered, embitterment may lead them to lash out wildly. This is the more likely to happen at a time when the whole Third World is in the throes of a revolution of rising expectations, and it may happen the more quickly if many hold high hopes of independence, but find these are disappointed. Both political parties recognize the danger. Both are thus committed to a policy of

improving the Fijians' position: any argument will be about the means rather than the end.

36. Whether the policy will succeed is another matter. Doubts must assail even the warmest admirer of the Fijian people, and they have never lacked admirers. This may indeed have been their undoing. Big genial men with huge smiles, ready courtesy and natural dignity, they are physically courageous and captivate men who meet them. But they have at the same time a deep pride in their own culture, an appreciation of the value of leisure and a childlike trust in others, all of which has tended to arouse protective instincts. Some have thus felt that they should be comfortably wrapped in a cocoon: treatment they have welcomed. So they remain, and have perhaps been encouraged to remain, accustomed to look for leadership to others, particularly to their Chiefs (whose authority is still immense), rather than to exercise much individual initiative. Changes in attitude will not come easily to them.

37. This need not be a cause for dismay: traditional societies are often stable and cohesive. But it probably means that much will depend upon whether the economy expands particularly fast. If it does, the Fijians may be swept along rapidly enough to allow possible discontent even though they do not catch up much on other races.

38. The prospects of its doing so look hopeful. Tourism is booming at a phenomenal rate, almost doubling in size every three years. Moreover it is labour intensive; it attracts large-scale capital investment; and it provides many fringe benefits. It will of course bring its own problems. Fortunately the dangers are appreciated in particular by Mara, and there is every sign that development will be controlled in a sensible manner. Mineral exploration during the last year or so has shown promising results and mining developments may well provide a substantial increase in job opportunities and in much needed infrastructure in the interior of the main islands. And forestry continues to show great long-term promise; a pulp industry now seems a likely starter.

39. A recent World Bank Mission to Fiji revealed a similar conclusion about prospects. It recorded a view that the country 'will enter Independence on a firmer economic base than many new countries. Balance of payment problems have been avoided and equilibrium should not be difficult to maintain. Minimal foreign borrowing has kept public debt service ratios low and debt service on private account is not significant. Debt service ratios in 1975 are estimated at 3 per cent of commodity exports and 1.3 per cent of non-factory export receipts for goods and services, the difference indicating the importance of tourism. Fiji can be considered creditworthy for Bank lending on its own account, following Independence'.

40. Moreover the strategy contained in Development Plan VI (to cover 1971–75) appears sound. For the economy as a whole the projected growth in domestic

produce is 6.9 per cent a year. This compares with 5 per cent annually over the last five years, during which there was a much higher rate in 1968–70 than in 1966–67. Tourism is expected to be the leading sector with an annual growth rate of 25 per cent, and emphasis is also to be placed on export growth and import substitution. Investment is projected to grow at more than 10 per cent per annum, exceeding 32 per cent of Gross National Product in 1975.

41. Emphasis is also rightly to be placed on rural development — on bringing the income of the population in the country areas, where incidentally most Fijians live, closer to that of town dwellers, and on providing those areas with better services so that they will be an attractive place to live. It is hoped thus to stop the drift to the towns and the consequent growth of a large urban unemployed class, many of them Fijians in a strange environment, cut off from their village roots: the increase in crime by young Fijians is already causing concern.

42. The plan is ambitious. The growth rate may prove a little beyond the country's capacity when viewed in the perspective of past performance. Furthermore the present high rate of private investment will be difficult to maintain. The construction sector in particular appears to have been reaching capacity in the last two years, so that further expansion will be difficult in the short run.

43. Whether the plan can be implemented in full will partly depend on what outside assistance is available. So I end with a brief look at an independent Fiji's likely international interests, hopes and attitudes. As an isolated archipelago, she will not be troubled by defence problems. Her immediate concern will be with neighbouring South Pacific Islands. Mara would undoubtedly like to be regarded as their leader, but is very conscious that others are jealous of Fiji and that he must be careful. He will probably continue to work for regional co-operation wherever possible, offering help where he can (for instance in training), hoping to increase trade and perhaps trying to coordinate some economic activities. I am sure he has no present ideas of any political confederation, however loose; nor should I regard one as a starter in the foreseeable future.

44. He will enjoy playing a part on a wider stage too, when Fiji joins the United Nations and the Commonwealth. But I expect it to be a cautious part. He has already shown that he would prefer to avoid taking sides — between Israel and the Arab States, between the two Chinas, and so on. Caution comes naturally to him: it is symptomatic that rather than inherit all Treaties unexamined on independence (signing a blank cheque ... he said) he has arranged for advice from an Australian Professor of International Law, so that an effective exercise can be done. Moreover he is unlikely to wish to be permanently aligned with any group, and Fiji is more likely than most new Commonwealth nations to be

open to argument about, and prepared to take a line helpful to the U.K. on, colonial issues at New York.

45. Partly as the result of encouragement from India, he has become involved with bodies like ECTFE and the Asian Bank, and has shown interest in the Colombo Plan. Links with India seem certain to be developed, even though there is not yet to be a Fiji High Commissioner in New Delhi. London and Canberra alone have been chosen, probably because most is expected of the UK and of Australia by way of trade and aid. For the UK here there is a great store of goodwill. This will not prevent Mara from the occasional display of bad temper when denied his way, but it should generally ensure a lasting and valued relationship.

46. Relations with Australia may be more difficult. Many here consider that the Australian Government has a large debt to repay, because Fiji has been exploited by big business from there and that official Australian attitudes are too often overbearing when they are not indifferent. These attitudes are in fact gradually changing, as is the Fijian view of Australia. But it is to be hoped that change will become rapid and radical enough to ensure much greater mutual understanding: Fiji certainly needs Australian interest and support.

47. From New Zealand she can look forward to getting both, although she will have no High Commission in Wellington. For there has long been close sympathy between the two countries, and this should continue to survive the occasional difference of view.

48. All in all, therefore the outlook is bright. There are certainly problems, but everyone is united in a genuine desire to solve them. There is not yet any real feeling of nationhood, but there is a solid core of goodwill and genuine tolerance which is a sounder basis than many emerging countries have had at the start of the journey. Above all Fiji is a country of common sense, and that is no small asset. Those of us here who have seen other countries at the same stage are at one in believing that things should go well.

49. It is perhaps not without significance that with the willing agreement of all concerned, the Union Flag will be lowered for the last time not as part of the Independence Parade on the 10th but, with the dignity which befits the departure of an old and respected friend, at a special Retreat ceremony on the evening before. In addition the new flag to be raised on the 10th incorporates the Union Flag.

www.ingramcontent.com/pod-product-compliance
Lightning Source LLC
Chambersburg PA
CBHW060947170426
43197CB00031B/2992